MW00426652

About the Author...

Authentic. What you see is what you get. Unpretentious and in your space for a purpose, are just a few of the words and statements that come to mind when thinking of Sharon Gregory. She is a dependable, get it done person with a heart of excellence leading her. Multi-gifted, yet in humility, she stays in her lanes of strength, which makes for a productive undertaking. Her life is a beautiful tapestry woven of love, support, justice and truth! Anything she touches is gold and will succeed.

~ Arlette Lanae'
Transformational Specialist & Author

It is with the greatest joy that I boast a bit, regarding **Sharon R. Gregory**. A tremendously, *loyal confidant, and trusted comrade.* She opens her mouth, and "WOW", rivers of living water begin to flow! I felt honored when she graced my life, decades ago. Sharon's insight to Life & Godliness, brought both, times of refreshing & challenge to my life; as well as others journeying, together with us.

I've admired Sharon, for her *commitment* to God. *Her honor for leaders*, and love for people, charitable works, and undoubtedly, family. Sharon is an *avid learner,* with a *sharp mind.* A *creative person, writer & instructor*; prone to ignite fire that inspires and make better! I know her as a *Leader* who serves *capably,* with *humility, respect and integrity.* Her s*ensitivity* to speak a word - **[God's Word]**, *in the right season* is remarkable! - *"Expect to know & to grow with Sharon R. Gregory!" - I have!*

Kimberly A. Colding-Claxton,
Visionary & Lead Creative Writer

KACO-Silverlining Literature

Affectionately known as Lady Kim ☺

My experience of Ms. Sharon Gregory is that of a woman of tremendous joy. She is a woman of dedication and great grace. She is extremely faithful. When she makes a commitment, she will move the Heavens and earth to keep her word and do her very best to complete her promise. For me, I can say that I have never had a more faithful and loving friend than Sharon. She has become my sister and is permanently etched into my heart and life forever! I am so very proud of her and all that she has accomplished. She has proven, as women, at any age, we can accomplish anything when given the opportunity.

~ A friend and sister for life, Prophetess Denise DeMaire

I knew from the moment she looked at me with a straight face and said, "You asked me out, right?" that I had just encountered someone very special, unique, different, but better yet, real. Although I was blown back by her response, the realness of her character enticed me all the more. I knew she was an interesting breed and I loved it! She is the realest, passionate, committed soldier for Jesus Christ I have ever met in my life. I am honored and truly blessed that God allowed our paths to cross. I never thought I would have the opportunity to not only meet, but also befriend someone that TRULY loves and obeys God as much as I do at the cost of everything...even our own lives. She is someone who KNOWS the fellowship of His suffering, as well as the power of His resurrection. She is someone who knows what it means to be a TRUE ambassador for Christ, as well as a TRUE friend. She is someone who can stand firm in the face of fear and not coward down or back out. She is someone who sees the enemy as he really is...small and insignificant. Sharon is someone who has been raised up in Him from her childhood, and truly knows God as Father. She is someone FULL of faith and doesn't waiver at the signs of what appears to be impossible. She is someone FULL of the Holy Ghost and not ashamed to proclaim His name wherever she goes. Furthermore, she is someone who sincerely believes that God is in control and He alone has the final say. I thank God for Sharon always. There's no other person I'd rather be with on this battlefield taking territory for Christ than she. For His Glory we will do it! Much love to you.

~Prophetess Tamika Morrow, Daughter of The King

THE

MAKING

OF

A

MILLION*HEIR*

*"It's not what you have; but rather what's inside
of you."*
St. Luke 12:15

Table of Contents

Publisher
C. J. Loray Media Group
Clarice L. Johnson
Senior Editor/Publisher
Sterling Heights, Michigan
586.843.4161

Cover Design
The HMG Agency
L'Oreal Hartwell
Saginaw, Michigan
810.210.2336

ISBN - 9781076014979

All scripture taken from KJV unless specified otherwise.

PREFACE

The priceless wisdom that no amount of money can compare. That jewel *in the making* that no amount of money can buy…It's in His presence. You can't put a price on what you receive from Him.

So many people are trying to get *"there,"* to the status of a Millionaire; but *"there"* **is found in prayer!** *"There"* **is in His presence**…the very place we've gotten away from. The place of peace. The place where the birthing of instruction, direction and clarity is brought forth. The place where the richness of everything needed is found. Where all things are revealed. The very place of PROSPERITY!

The secret place in which "The Making of a Million*heir*" is *taking place.* The Million*heir* is *being made!* *"There"* is where I quietly heard this in my spirit and where the Holy Spirit began to illuminate to me, that I may write and share with you, that whatever you want to be, whatever you are striving for, whatever your purpose, your posture or your position, it is *"there"* in prayer, and in His presence that *you* are made!

During the onset of this book, more began to be revealed to me. As I would just write, weep, and pray that what the Lord was sharing with me would be shared worldwide, penetrating the hearts of many, as there becomes a greater hunger to be "rich" in the knowledge of Him!

More than a decade has expired since the initial year in which the Lord arrested my spirit with the title and the miraculous writing of this book. My hands literally shook as I wrote endlessly without fail, which was an experience I never witnessed before. However, it was in the rewriting, and coming to understand what it was I had written, and the real work it would take to properly get the book done, that brought me to this long, delayed year of publication. I share this to let other writers out there know that His grace *truly* is sufficient for us. He knows each of our day's challenges, struggles, disappointments, discouragements, and our very own **inexcusable** reasons why we haven't done what it is He has given and placed in all His children to do.

MY THANKS...

Thanks be unto GOD who has caused me to TRIUMPH in all things!

I Love YOU

Thanks to my precious jewel, that was actually still and quiet long enough to help make this happen (smile).

Love you, Babe

Thanks to a mom like no other! Especially when you and your grand child get together (smile).
Anyone who know us, know what I mean!
The reality of *that* combination and *this* book coming together let's me know "*I can* do all things through Christ who strengtheneth me."

Love you, Mom

Thanks to all my "*family*" in Christ who kept me encouraged and convinced of all of the God given abilities on the inside of me.

Love you

MY PRAYER

I pray this book blesses the lives of all who read it.

I pray you do prosper and be in health...

I pray according to His purpose...

I pray after the council of His will!!!

WHEN YOU PRAY...SHUT THE DOOR

It's when no one sees it...No one realizes... No one recognizes...That quiet time...The personal time. The time that the world and the things of this world have almost *snatched* away from many of us.

The hustle. The bustle. The business of family, work, work, and then more work! It seems as though work in the corporate world has replaced much of what America used to value as *"family time,"* dinner time, rest and relaxation. When we're not working, we're finding more work to replace what time we could have.

Let's look at a passage in scripture that describes the very thing mentioned. I pray it causes us to see differently everything we are faced with, making wise decisions towards that end on what is needful on a day to day basis.

In the Gospel according to Luke, chapter 10, starting at verse 38, it reads as followed...

"Now it came to pass, as they went, that He entered into a certain village: and a certain woman named Martha received Him into her

house. And she had a sister named Mary who seated herself at the Lord's feet and was listening to His teaching. But Martha [overly occupied and too busy] was distracted with much serving; and she came up to Him and said, Lord, is it nothing to You that my sister has left me to serve alone"? (Amplified Bible)

Let's interject to focus in on a few of the above scriptures. For Martha to imply Jesus' care regarding her sister having "left" her to serve alone, could safely suggest, at some point, she was up helping, but recognized the importance of leaving everything else to receive the word of God.

In order to appreciate what is taking place here, we must look intently into the task that Martha received unto herself. In reading verse 38, the word *"they"* possibly included the twelve disciples from verse 38, the lawyer who may have followed from verse 25, the seventy from when they were sent out and returned from verse 17, not to mention the chance of the "much" people that met Him in chapter 9, verse 37. There may be numerous thoughts…all these people in one house? Remember, Jesus often had crowds wherever He went. So, no matter the number, imagine the weight of work Martha *could* have had.

Let's continue...

"Tell her then to help me [to lend a hand and do her part along with me]! But the Lord replied to her by saying, "Martha, Martha, you are anxious and troubled about many things; There is need of only one. Mary has chosen the good portion [that which is to her advantage], which shall not be taken away from her."
(Amplified Bible)

Now at this point, cold, heartless and uncaring as it may sound, Jesus takes notice of the things we do, and is aware of the choices we make that take precedence over Him. One thing stands clear, He is NOT impressed with us just *"being busy!"*

As prompted to begin this section with Matthew 6:6, "When You Pray...Shut the Door," it dawned on me how *much* has entered into our lives. A vast number of people are cumbered about, in various applications, with much "serving." Whether man or machine; jobs or family; television or computer, we have failed to choose that which is needful. So, like Martha, we find ourselves troubled, peering out at others, and like the children of Israel, on endless journeys and cycles of "wanderings and wondering." We begin wondering where our lives are going...Wondering if anything we're doing is really worth it, or whether it's all in vain. We begin wandering to and fro, back and forth, tossed with every wind and doctrine, confused, changing beliefs, religions and churches in the manner we change clothes. We rise early. We stay up late, needing more, receiving less. We put in time needed to get someplace, but never arrive, wondering how others are ahead and we're still behind.

The bible reminds us that hell and destruction are never full; so the eyes of man are never satisfied, according to Proverbs 27:20. Therefore, if our hearts really are in THE KING's hand, as also stated in Proverbs, then only until we turn our hearts towards Him, choose what is needful, and allow Him to fill us, we'll continue laboring in our own strength, never coming into a true place of satisfaction.

Let's look into another passage of scripture in Romans chapter 6, verse 12, which reads, *"Let not sin therefore reign in your mortal body, that ye should obey it [the sin] in the lusts thereof."* *[What the sin desires or wants you to do to fulfill its appetite; what it's longing for.]*

Verse 21 reads, *"What fruit had ye then in those things whereof ye are now ashamed? For the end of those things [is] death."* What can you show for it? What do you have from it?

This passage of scripture speaks regarding sins past, present and future! Things done that we should not talk about, nor may *want* to discuss. In comparison, we should equally be ashamed working countless hours, yielding little to no fruit, while the structure of the family unit suffers continuously. The role of father and mother is rapidly replaced in children's upbringing by the television and the internet. Likewise, marriage is rarely the honorable thing as husbands and wives undo vows as quick as they say, "I do," endure not until the end, and play it, as it were, a game of chance.

James, Chapter 4 asks a question that gives the answer. *"What leads to strife (discord and feuds) and how do conflicts (quarrels and fights) originate among you? Do they not arise from your sensual desires that are ever warring in your bodily members? You are jealous and covet [what others have] and your desires go unfulfilled; [so] you become murderers. [To hate is to murder as far as your hearts are concerned.] You burn with envy and anger and are not able to obtain [the gratification, the contentment, and the happiness that you seek], so you fight and war. You do not have, because you do not ask. [Or] you do ask [God for them] and yet fail to receive, because you ask with wrong purpose and evil, selfish motives. Your intention is [when you get what you desire] to spend it in sensual pleasures. You [are like] unfaithful wives [having illicit love affairs with the world and breaking your marriage vow to God]."* (Amplified Bible)

The word **"Desire,"** (another word for lust), in its simplest definition, is nothing but an *intense* longing (for anything). Something *craved.* A **deep driven** *hunger* for that which is desired, until obtained. Whether a home, career, position or status, we have allowed what we desire to take precedence over what is needful. Desire (or lust) has destroyed, at an alarming rate, men of integrity and has caused the worth once valued in women to become compromised at whatever cost. Desire has consumed our very reason for being until we've become cumbered about with what we want. We will stop at nothing (no matter the cost) to get it.

Remember, **we** make up the Church, and as long as *we allow* lust to drive us in its direction, **we** will *NEVER* be the Body that Christ *intended,* doing the *"things"* that God *purposed*! We have s*hut* the door to opportunities to know Him. We have s*hut* the door to chances of finding out answers to various problems related to family, finance and future.

Imagine the possibilities, if the same amount of energy we placed in the desires of the flesh…to obey it in the lusts thereof, was exerted in the word of God, to obey it. God's desire is for us to *want* to be in His presence. His desire is for us to *want* to spend time with Him. For He desires that we prosper and be in health, even as our souls prosper (3rd John v.2). He *longs* for it!

I invite you… "*Shut the door*," and enter into a world of prayer.

I invite you...enter into a lifestyle of peace and prosperity.

Experience an atmosphere of things that can only come when we realize we have been doing much of the wrong "things." We have done little of the only thing it is going to take to turn our lives, the lives of our children and the state of this world back in the right direction!

*…Are you choosing the **Needful** things?*

RICHES UNTOLD

As I heard, "The Making of a Million*heir*," a whole new revelation unfolded right before me. I cannot emphasize it enough. It is there you are being *made*, right in the presence of an ALMIGHTY GOD…In your secret place with the Most High!

I tell you of a truth, no amount of money can be placed on the making of a *true millionaire*! What we possess inward, and all of what is being put in you that is coming out of you, making you who you really are.

Let's look again in the Word of God, in the Gospel of St. Luke, chapter 12, staring at verse 15…

> *"And He said unto them, "Take heed [listen intently; watch; be careful], and beware of covetousness: for a man's life consisteth not in the abundance of the things which he possesseth."*

Now, oftentimes, we get off of the word by shortening scripture in order to have opportunity for input. You will find throughout the entirety of this book I have chosen to write out scripture. I, too, desire that you be *"full"* of the word of God, that ye may grow thereby. What safer place to be than in His presence *and* in His word (another needful thing)!

The Bible makes reference to Eve in Genesis 3:6. *"And when the woman **saw** that the tree was good...and that it was pleasant...and a tree to be desired to make one wise, she took...and did **eat**, and **gave** also..."*

Now, based upon what it is you're **looking** at, and *your view* of how good and pleasant it is *to you*, will determine your drive to take and eat at the level and cost of that drive, lust or desire. Here, Adam and Eve *ate* to their own destruction! What would happen if we ate of that which was good? What if we tasted from that which was pleasant, gave to those who were with us, then watched the effect and impact it left on a people and in a world by giving LIFE and not death; GROWTH, and not a stunt thereof; EXPANSION and PRODUCTIVITY, and not deprivation and desolation.

I desire that you taste *and* see that the word is good, that it is pleasant. I pray that you desire it more and more, for the word of God makes one wise. It increases you and it builds you up. It strengthens you...So, do eat, by all means...any means, give also to others who may not have, who, perhaps may not quite understand. Watch their lives, as well as yours, grow to proportions of which you know not!

Don't forget…"Read*** the word; ***eat*** the word; ***give*** the word away!" (Give me credit first, and then run with it…Smile!)

Let's continue in Luke (12:16)

> ***"And He spake a parable unto them, saying, "The ground of a certain rich man brought forth plentifully: And he thought within himself, saying, What shall I do, because I have no room where to bestow my fruits."***

Now, it's evident here that as we work, we gain. But, let us not think that all gain is godliness, especially when it is consumed to one's self in the wrong spirit, for the wrong purpose, in the wrong manner, for the wrong intent!

> ***"And he said, This will I do: I will pull down my barns, and build greater; and there will I bestow all my fruits and my goods."***

> *Make sure you are not building simply for the sake of "saying" how much you have or how much you have done.*

> ***"And I will say to my soul, Soul, thou hast much goods laid up for many years; take thine ease, eat, drink, and be merry."***

Deuteronomy 8:11-19, emphasis on verse 12-14, 17 and 19 says,

> *"Beware that thou forget not the Lord thy God...Lest when thou hast eaten and are full, and hast built goodly houses...and thy silver and thy gold is multiplied, and all that thou hast is multiplied; Then thine heart be lifted up, and thou forget the Lord thy God...And thou say in thine heart, My power and the might of mine hand hath gotten me this wealth...And it shall be, if thou do at all forget...that ye shall surely perish. (KJV)*

Continuing in Luke 12:20...

> *"But God said unto him, Thou fool, this night thy soul shall be required of thee: then whose shall those things be, which thou hast provided?"*
> *(KJV)*

I want to sidebar for a second. I would like to bring attention to the second "soul" above in verse 19 of Luke, and how it is capitalized in scripture. I would dare, and think it safe to say that, that was the same spirit of haughtiness and lifting up of self, because of what he had, that caused Lucifer to become *full of himself*; get beside himself, and begin to think that what he had, he acquired on his own, which resulted in him being *shot* (like a lightening bolt) out of Heaven!

The scripture goes on to say in verse 21…

"So is he that layeth up treasure for himself and is not rich toward God." [Likewise, in the same way, the same thing will happen.]

Read that a few times until you *see* that the person who is laying up treasure for himself *is doing it,* however, *is NOT rich*! In referencing the above scripture, the Spirit of the Lord allowed me to see that what we consider treasure and "things" stored up that define us as *rich* is **NOT** what He considers rich. According to this, what God is saying to us is, See if you can lay up something for yourself, not be rich towards Me, and you not see it taken away from you. See if you can actually obtain, yet, be in deception in thinking you have accomplished something. People of God, there is *"evil treasure"* and *"good treasure"* (Matthew 12:35). There is *"success"* and *"good success"* (Joshua 1:18). There is *"our way"* and *"God's way"* (Isiah 55:8; Proverbs 14:12).

More word to the wise…since God has made foolish the wisdom of *this world,* you **will** and **can** be deceived into believing you have it made, only to look around in disappointment, finding that you were nowhere *in,* or *close* to the will of God, nor His intent for your life. *"And I will say to my soul, Soul, thou hast much goods laid up for many years; take thine ease, eat, drink, and be merry." Luke 12:19.*

We often find ourselves becoming the by-product, or the result of this, and similar references in scripture. When it comes to *"knowing"* what God's will is, and *"how"* to go about obtaining it, only He knows the **way** to take. There is a very fine line we can find ourselves crossing when trying to reach **God's goals through the mindset of man**.

We believe money and things are what give us our definition in life. The more we have of it, the better off we'll be. Then, why so much suicide? Why so much hatred? Why so much murder? Why so many wars within ourselves and amongst each other? James 4:1-3 says, *"From whence come wars and fightings among you? Come they not hence, even of your lusts (desires) that war (fight you) in your members (within you; your inner struggles)? Ye lust, and have not: ye kill, and desire to have, and cannot obtain: ye fight and war, yet ye have not, because ye ask not. Ye ask and receive not, because ye ask amiss, that ye may consume it upon your lusts.*

We believe the more we have, the better the person will be. Then why such a change in character? Why so much separation? Why so much divorce? Infidelity?

At the onset of "The Making of a Million*heir*," the word "*making*" continued to stand out.

The Spirit of The Lord **NEVER** stopped reiterating that "*within*" a true million*heir*, the "*making*" **never** ceases. It's a **constant** and **continuous** work. We, however, have confused the "*state*" of being with the "*status*" of being, due to the pressures we have allowed the world and its "systems" to place on us, the Body of Christ. This is it… so we think. This is what places me amongst the "*Who's who in society,*" so we thought.

People literally think that money is what "makes" us millionaires, when the *process* of us becoming anything valuable in life, is a lifetime of priceless deposits that no amount of money could ever do!

- ➤ The priceless gift of The Holy Ghost that has been *given* us

- ➤ Christ "*in*" us, the Hope of Glory

- ➤ Virtue *bestowed* upon us by our mothers, both natural and spiritual

- ➤ The millions of countless words *spoken* over us that grounded us and gave us the foundation we *now* stand in

- ➤ The Apostles who helped *establish* us

- ➤ The Prophets who saw beyond what broke us down, in order to *build* us back up again

- ➤ The Pastors who nourished, and nurtured, handled us with care, and *cared* for us

- ➤ The Teachers who *taught* endlessly to make sure we had it; understood it; kept it, and walked it out, and last, but definitely not least...

- ➤ The Evangelists, who got down in the dirt with us, and did what it took to *bring* us up *out of* that thing

That's the "*Making*" of a *true* Million*heir*, the *making to which* God is referring. He's making you the value of who you are *on the inside*, bringing out of you, over the course of an entire lifetime, the value of what could never be counted in pockets or in bank accounts.

In today's world, I believe it's safe to say, most people are trying to "*make*" money, "b*ring*" wealth, and "*heap*" riches to themselves (Psalms 75: 6, 7 says, ***"For promotion cometh neither from the east, nor from the west, nor from the south. But God is judge: He putteth down one, and setteth up another."***

I can hear someone saying, "Well, money sure does help!" It sure does, Beloved. After all, money answereth all things, according to Ecclesiastes 10:19. Money, while it has been, and remains one of the main resources in the earth, was given that we may establish God's Kingdom in the earth and spread the Gospel of Jesus Christ.

"But thou shalt remember the Lord thy God: for it is He that giveth thee power to get wealth, that He may establish His covenant which He sware unto thy fathers, as it is this day."
(Deuteronomy 8:18)

And he said unto them, "Go ye into all the world, and preach the gospel to every creature."
(Mark 16:15)

Money is our *ability* to buy, sell, and trade in the marketplace. However, as it is properly written in 1 Timothy 6:10, the *love* of this same commodity has become the root of all evil. *"For the love of money is the root of all evil: which while some coveted after, they have erred from the faith, and pierced themselves through with many sorrows."*

It has been the *love* of money that has caused massive destruction, endless hurt, meaningless deaths, countless divisions, astronomical debt, and a shameful amount of loss in integrity, character, and trust!

Ecclesiastes 10:19 says, *"A feast is made for laughter, and wine maketh merry: but money answereth all things."* The word *"things"* in this particular scripture is italicized, which infers in the original writing of text, it was *not* there. So, while money answereth all, it's not *the answer*! Though it may be given as a *means* to an end, given at the time to aide and assist, it **cannot** be given to get to the root of a situation and deal with the source from whence it came.

Let *us,* therefore, make sure *we* are not amongst those whose *"love for it"* leads in the way of evil. 1 Timothy 6:9, 10 says, *"But they that will be rich fall into temptation and a snare, and into many foolish and hurtful lusts, which drown men in destruction and perdition. For the love of money is the root of all evil: which while some coveted after, they have erred from the faith, and pierced themselves through with many sorrows."*

Luke. 8:14 says, *"And that which fell among thorns are they, which, when they have heard, go forth, and are choked with cares and riches and pleasures of this life, and bring no fruit to perfection."*

2 Timothy 3:4 says, *"Traitors, heady, highminded, lovers of pleasures more than lovers of God."*

Instead, while ***being made*** and ***becoming rich*** *within* and *without*, let us remain lovers of God, seeking first ***His*** kingdom and ***His*** righteousness that we may enter into the *true* riches of the Lord, eat from the *true* good of the land, and have all things added unto us…indeed.

The Word of God is one thing we ***must*** keep before us in order to know what to do and what's best! 1 Timothy 6:11, 17-19 conveys, ***"But thou, O man of God, flee these things; and follow after righteousness, godliness, faith, love, patience, meekness…Charge them that are rich in this world, that they be not high-minded, nor trust in uncertain riches, but in The Living God, who giveth us richly all things to enjoy; That they do good, that they be rich in good works, ready to distribute, willing to communicate; Laying up in store for themselves a good foundation against the time to come, that they may lay hold on eternal life."***

*...**Who** and **What** are **you** rich towards?*

THE LOVE OF MONEY

It is not the actual medium of money that I'm against. However, it is what the *love* of it has caused many to compromise. And when it is a *must* to have, we'll find ourselves going to **any measure** to get it at the cost of losing what's much more valuable.

Some may say, "*You do what you have to do!*" That may be the case for some. But, may I remind you, it has been that attitude that has us where we are today. Not to mention the loss of morals and values that we, as a people held to in times past, and respected for years! At this point, I would like each of us to ask ourselves this question, "Have I stopped or even had the time to stop long enough to ask God what it is He desires for my life? In which direction has He destined me to go?

We give thought to the job we want, the location we desire it to be in, and the positions for which we are striving. We determine *beforehand* the money bracket in which it **must** fall in order to even consider the job. On the same note, how many of us give as *equally* as much thought and time to "becoming rich" in *spiritual things* as we do in *natural things*?

Job 14:5 reminds us that our days are already determined and our way appointed that no man can pass [get around; get by]. "Seeing his days are determined, the number of his months are with thee, thou hast appointed his bounds that he cannot pass. He cannot pass. It is already *purposed*! It is already *set*! So, it would *behoove* us as students to simply ask the teacher. As sons and daughters, we should ask The Father. As creation, it is our duty to ask **The Creator** who, by the way, is more knowledgeable regarding the problem and the path to its solution.

Unfortunately, some would rather continue in *their own way* when help is as close as **an extension of the hand, an opening of the mouth, a turning of the heart**. We have been so accustomed to trying to "*do it ourselves*," that we tell ourselves we don't need any help. We have *convinced* ourselves we can handle it on our own…right? Then why have we made such a mess of our lives? Why do we have so much trouble in and around our communities? Why so much debt? Why are we so disgusted? Why do we find ourselves in frustration as often as we do?

Jeremiah 10:23 says, ***"O Lord, I know that the way of man is not in himself: it is not in man that walketh to direct his steps."***

Herein lies my questions…if it is **NOT** in man to direct his steps, and it is **NOT** in man to know his own way, and it is definitely **NOT** in him to know what's best or needful, **HOW** are we doing so much on our own without seeking the face of God?! How have we gotten so messed up, so confused and so deceived all at the same time? We have EVERYTHING, so we think, and possess nothing. We're still miserable. We're not satisfied. We're empty and still searching for something we're not quite able to put our finger on, and so begins the *"cycle"* of *wanderings* and *wondering* all over again into things that has profited us nothing. It has gotten us nowhere even faster!

We have EVERYTHING *under control* while everything is spiraling *out of control* right before our very eyes. Whether we've grown accustomed to it, become numbed by it, allowed society to lullaby us to sleep, or simply turned our backs on it, we're still responsible for it.

"I am speaking in familiar human terms because of your natural limitations. For as you yielded your bodily members [and faculties] as servants to impurity and ever-increasing lawlessness, so now yield your bodily members [and faculties] once for all as servants to righteousness (right being and doing) [which leads] to sanctification. For when you were slaves of sin, you were free, in regards to righteousness. But, then what benefit (return) did you get from the things of which you are now ashamed? [None] for the end of those things is death. But now since you have been set free from sin and have become the slaves of God, you have your present reward in holiness and its end is eternal life. For the wages which sin pays is death, but the [bountiful] free gift of God is eternal life through (in union with) Jesus Christ our Lord."
Romans 6:19-23 (Amplified Bible)

Our hearts have been towards so much in the past that we have lost focus and track of what is really important and what really matters. Let us all <u>now</u> begin to refocus and turn our hearts back towards the One who has given to us all things *richly* to enjoy for His purpose and His glory only. After all, *"For where your treasure is, there will your heart be also." (Luke 12:34)*

*…**Where** are you and **What** are you after?*

FOR WHAT DOES IT *PROFIT?*

So far, we have covered a great amount of ground and a wealth of information according to the word of God. Let's look further into more scriptures to go deeper into "The Making of a Million*Heir*," concerning the "whole matter."

Luke, Chapter 12, beginning at verse 22 reads, *"And he said unto his disciples, Therefore I say unto you, Take no thought for your life, what ye shall eat; neither for the body, what ye shall put on."*

We'll pause here for a moment to consider if we really believe God. Matthew 15:8 says, *"This people draweth near unto Me with their mouth, and honoreth Me with their lips; but their heart is far from Me."*

If we really took no thought for our lives, less of us, especially us who profess Christ, would be *"conformed"* to this world, and more of us would be *transformed* to know what is *His* will. *"And be not conformed to this world: but be ye transformed by the renewing of your mind, that ye may prove what is that good, and acceptable, and perfect, will of God." (Romans 12:2)*

We would be prospering or *producing* results in the things of God, having confidence that our Father knows of what *"things"* we have need. In verse 29 of the same Chapter (Luke 12: 22-34), it assures us not to be of a *"doubtful"* mind. ***"And seek not ye what ye shall eat, or what ye shall drink, neither be ye of <u>doubtful</u> mind."***

Verse 30 reads, ***"For all these "things" do the nations of the world seek after: and your Father knoweth that ye have need of these "things."*** May I remind you that we are not of this world? ***"I have given them thy word; and the world hath hated them, because they are not of the world, even as I am not of the world." (John 17:14)***

Luke 12:31, ***"But rather seek ye the kingdom of God; and all these things shall be added unto you."*** Verse 31 informs us rather to *"seek"* (to go in search of; to look for; try to discover, acquire or gain; aim at; make an attempt). This very passage infers that ***it is going to take some time***. It also suggests to me that if we are told to seek, either something has been lost and there is an *attempt* and *chance* to gain it back, or something **needs** to be **sought after,** because it has, under false perceptions, never been obtained in *the way intended.*

It took some time for us to get it the way *we've* done it for so long. Now, I challenge each of us to take the time to undo it *"our way"* and seek the Kingdom of God (God's way of doing it). Surely all things shall…not might, not maybe…but *all things* shall be added unto you.

You can continue in the way that you have been going, or you can make a conscious decision to do it God's way. Proverbs 16:25 reminds us that ***"There is a way that seemeth right unto a man, but the end thereof are the ways of death."*** In the Hebrew, the word ***"death"*** means it can be literal or figurative. Here, we will go with its definition of actual ruin. The choice is yours. I'll give the advice of Our Father, as well as any other loving parent: choose life! Deuteronomy 30:15-20 conveys, ***"See, I have set before thee this day life and good, and death and evil; In that I command thee this day to love the Lord thy God, to walk in His ways, and to keep His commandments, and His statutes and His judgments, that thou mayest live and multiply: and the Lord thy God shall bless thee in the land whither thou goest to possess it. But if thine heart turn away, so that thou wilt not hear, but shalt be drawn away, and worship other gods, and serve them; I denounce unto you this day that ye shall surely perish, and that ye shall not prolong your days upon the land…I call heaven and earth to record this day against you, that I have set before you life and***

41

death, blessing and cursing: therefore choose life, that both thou and thy seed may live: That thou mayest love the Lord thy God, and that thou mayest obey His voice, and that thou mayest cleave unto Him: For He is thy life, and the length of thy days."

In the gospel according to Mark, Chapter 8, starting at verse 36, it reads, *"For what shall it profit a man, if he shall gain the whole world, <u>and</u> lose his own soul?"* Again, **you will gain**, but *ultimately* **you lose** if your heart is not towards God and the *"things"* of God. All gain *is not* good! I Timothy 4:7-10 states, *"...and exercise thyself rather unto godliness...godliness is profitable unto all things, having promise of the life that now is, and of that which is to come. This is a faithful saying and worthy of all acceptation. For therefore we both labor and suffer reproach, because we trust in the living God, who is the Savior of all men, specially of those that believe."*

Remember, we're talking about *true prosperity*...Prospering even as our souls prosper, or better yet, the *"Making"* of a Million*Heir*. If it is as our soul prospers, equal or according to, then we must not fail to look at the *"condition"* of the soul. What better place to start than the beginning?

Genesis 2:7 reads, *"And the Lord God formed man of the dust of the ground, and breathed into his nostrils the breath of life; and man became a living soul"* (you become based on what God has put in you, not society, not man).

Genesis 1:2 reads, *"And the earth was without form, and void." [empty; and we are considered "earth –en" vessels]*. The latter of the book of Acts 17:25 states, *"He giveth to all life, and breath, and all things."* Acts 17:28 reads, *"For in Him we live, and move, and have our being."* Finally, James 4:14-16 says, *"Whereas ye know not what shall be on the morrow. For what is your life? It is <u>even a vapor</u>, that appeareth for a little time, and then vanisheth away. For that ye ought to say, If the Lord will, we shall live, and do this, or that. But now ye rejoice in your <u>boastings</u>: all such rejoicing is evil."*

These scriptures clearly *state* and *allow us* **to see** that without God, we are empty on the inside, no matter how hard we work for it to appear otherwise on the outside. We are void and without hope in this world. We have nothing and can do nothing without Him *("…for without Me ye can do nothing." John 15:5).* He is the very source of our life, breath and being!

"And hath made of one blood all nations of men for to dwell on all the face of the earth, and hath determined the times before appointed, and the bounds of their habitation; That they should seek the Lord, if haply they might feel after him, and find him, though he be not far from every one of us." (Acts 17:26-27)

Let's continue in Genesis 1:2. *"And darkness was upon the face of the deep."* Here, darkness gives reference to another world, and the state of that world after the fall of Lucifer. In our discussion, I will use it in another sense. On the surface, and in the *face* of *"looking to par"* and holding it all together. These are the obvious affects that darkness and evil have on us, the *state* of our children, our marriages, our homes, and our *individual* worlds that spill over into the world in which we live.

Looking and acting to par is *not* remedy for what's really going on, deep within. If we asked ourselves, and were **honest**, we'd see the *true state* we're living in; the *true condition* of this darkness upon the *face* (exterior and interior). The extraordinary counter-reaction to this scripture and any given condition, such as this is that the Spirit of God *moved* upon…There's always a loving God *waiting* to move; *waiting* for opportunity to free, snatch out of darkness, and make whole.

How long has it been since the church of the *Living* God, the saints of the *Most-High* God, encountered a true *move* of the Spirit? I'm talking about a move that *affects* the very *depths* of society insomuch **they come** asking, *by what power, or by what name, are ye doing this? "And when they had set them in the midst, they asked, by what power, or by what name, have ye done this?" (Acts 4:7)*

I'm talking about a move insomuch as **they marvel** and take knowledge and can say nothing against it. I'm talking about a move insomuch as it causes as much a stir and acts as a conversation piece as the works of darkness.

Let's go back to Mark 8:36, *"For what doth it profit to gain…and lose your soul?"* The soul is the very "*seat*" of emotion. What does it profit to gain…and lose your peace of mind? What does it profit to gain…and lose your sense of stability? *"Riches profit not in the day of wrath: but righteousness delivereth from death." (Proverbs 11:4)*

We can continue pretending all we want, *gaining* what we will, while *losing* out on the very things that are of the utmost importance to God. What sense does it make to have everything you want and not have a balance in life? *"A false balance is an abomination to the Lord: but a just weight is his delight." (Proverbs 11:1)*

45

Since we are speaking of "Just Weights," why not have…

Your marriage unified as God intended:

"Marriage is honourable in all, and the bed undefiled: but whoremongers and adulterers God will judge." (Hebrews 13:4)

"For this cause shall a man leave his father and mother, and shall be joined unto his wife, and they two shall be one flesh. This is a great mystery: but I speak concerning Christ and the church." (Ephesians 5:31-32)

Your home properly ran:

"But if any provide not for his own, and specially for those of his own house, he hath denied the faith, and is worse than an infidel." (1 Timothy 5:8)

This is a true saying, if a man desire the office of a bishop, he desireth a good work. A bishop then must be blameless, the husband of one wife, vigilant, sober, of good behaviour, given to hospitality, apt to teach; Not given to wine, no striker, not greedy of filthy lucre; but patient, not a brawler, not covetous; One that ruleth well his own house, having his children in subjection with all gravity; (For if a man know not how to rule his own house, how shall he take care of the church of God?) Not a novice, lest being lifted up with pride he falls into the condemnation of the devil. Moreover, he must have a good report of them which are without; lest he fall into reproach and the snare of the devil." (1Timothy 3:1-7)

Your family stable:

"And if it seem evil unto you to serve the Lord, choose you this day whom ye will serve; whether the gods which your fathers served that were on the other side of the flood, or the gods of the Amorites, in whose land ye dwell: but as for me and my house, we will serve the Lord." (Joshua 24:15).

And, your soul secured in Him:

"For what shall it profit a man, if he shall gain the whole world, and lose his own soul." (Mark 8:36)

"For whosoever shall call upon the name of the Lord shall be saved." (Romans 10:13)

I'm reminded of the **POWER** the disciples walked in when confronted with what *seemed* to be various impossibilities.

"Then Peter said, 'Silver and gold have I none; but such as I have, give I thee: In the Name of Jesus Christ of Nazareth rise up and walk. I don't have any money; however, I do have the Name of Jesus! I have the Power of Jesus! I have the Authority of Jesus! I have the power to do what money can't! In the Name of Jesus Christ of Nazareth, rise up and walk."
(Acts 3:6-10)

RISE UP AND WALK child of God! Rise up and walk in the level of power and anointing that has been secured for us through Christ Jesus. Secure your family! Secure your inheritance in the kingdom! Secure your *rights* and *rank* in the Spirit! Secure your position that has *been given* by the shed blood of Jesus Christ!

"Rise up and walk, and secure the victory handed over to us in the triumph of Christ having spoiled principalities and powers, making a show of them openly." (Colossians 2:15)

You may not have all you want right now. But you definitely have been given all you need. Please, by no means, compromise and lose your soul, selling it short, for a bowl of soup and pleasure, *but for a season*!

"And Jacob sod pottage: and Esau came from the field, and he was faint: And Esau said to Jacob, Feed me, I pray thee, with that same red pottage; for I am faint: therefore was his name called Edom. And Jacob said, Sell me this day thy birthright. And Esau said, Behold, I am <u>at the point</u> to die: and what profit shall this birthright do to me? And Jacob said, <u>Swear</u> to me this day; and he sware unto him: and he sold his birthright unto Jacob. Then Jacob gave Esau bread and pottage of lentiles; and he did eat and drink, and rose up, and went his way: thus, Esau despised his birthright." (Gen 25:29-34)

"Choosing rather to suffer affliction with the people of God, than to enjoy the pleasures of sin for a season." (Hebrews 11:25)

Other Examples in Scripture of POWER Displayed

Acts 20:7-12 states, *"...Paul preached...and continued his speech until midnight. And there sat in a window a certain young man...being fallen into a deep sleep: and as Paul was long preaching, he sunk down with sleep and fell from the third loft, and was taken up dead, And Paul went down and fell on him, and embracing said, trouble not yourselves; for his life is in him."*

Now, that's **LIFE** more abundantly. That's more than what and how we know it to be today! Paul went back to what he was doing with NO concern and doubt.

Verse 12, "And they brought the young man ALIVE, and were not a little comforted."

They were not just comforted a little, rather the entire situation set them up for a greater *hunger*, *excitement* and **BELIEF** in the word of God. Not to mention, Paul who would have no trouble from that point on keeping the attention and hunger of the people in the things of God.

Mark 5:22-23, 35-42 "... there cometh a ruler...besought Him greatly, saying my little daughter lieth at the point of death. I pray thee come and lay thy hands...that she may be healed, and she shall live. While He yet spake...Thy daughter is dead: why troublest thou the Master any further...Be not afraid, only believe."

The ruler didn't offer a certain dollar amount for her life. He definitely had the money. He was a **Ruler**. Nevertheless, he **knew** it was *not* in the dollar, but in the power. How many have had the money and *it* could do NOTHING for you? How many of us have not only been troubled greatly, but have not been comforted regarding deaths, in a literal sense, or symbolically?

Let's continue along in this passage of Mark, verse 25, *"And a certain woman, which had an issue of blood twelve years, And had suffered many things of many physicians, and had spent all that she had, and was nothing bettered, but rather grew worse, When she had heard of Jesus...For she said, If I may touch but His clothes, I SHALL BE WHOLE. And straightway the fountain of her blood was dried up!"*

Remember, after a *true* encounter with Jesus, nothing remains the same, and straightway, without a *"step"* plan, you can experience a life change for the best. This woman had nothing to offer Jesus. In fact, she was the one in desperate need. And when you're in need, the *first thing* you look for is help. The *last thing* you expect is the drying up of resources and/or everything you have worked for so long in order to get that help. Many of us have no GREAT thing to offer Jesus. Nonetheless, as the woman portrayed in this scripture, many have suffered at the hands of others. We have looked for years for answers, only to come up empty and, at times, worse off than before.

If you would just BELIEVE. Offer Him your heart. With a ***total surrender*** in faith, you too, can touch the heart of the Father and cause many issues in your life to dry up today!

Mark 5:2-16 conveys, "...immediately there met Him (Jesus) a man with an unclean spirit...and no man could bind him...neither could any tame him."

As in this scripture, how many of us have *allowed* unclean things to enter our lives? Our homes? Our morals? Our values? How many of us have lost control of our children and *claim* we can no longer tame them, as if they're some wild animal, loosed without a trainer? It's up to us to ***"Train up a child in the way he should go," according to Proverbs 22:6.*** It's time to take our rightful positions as parents, and stop letting television, computers and games be their examples and role models.

Get out of the stress related two (2) to three (3) job holdings only to barely *"make ends meet,"* at the expense of losing our children and households. The more you have, the more you tend to spend. Let's get some DISCIPLINE with what is available and get back into the home.

Note: I go more into detail regarding this subject in the book the Lord has given me to write entitled, *"Who's Raising Who?"* Look for it on bookshelves everywhere!

Too many of us have lost control of our finances, family and future with little to no recourse of gaining it back.

Acts, Chapter 9, although excellent in its entirety, will be visited starting at verse 19, which says, *"...Ananias went his way...And immediately there fell from Saul's eyes as it had been scales: and he received sight forthwith, arose and was baptized."*

Your *past* position, and/or lifestyle, does not matter, people of God. What matters is your *present* position and *willingness* to **allow** the ability and very *"life-changing"* power of Jesus Christ to take you in a totally new direction.

Join the millions who have *received their sight*: new insight into the very mind, will, way and heart of the Father. Those who have arose from where they were to an overcoming power that has *"baptized"* (immersed) them into a belief that keeps them fighting *"The good fight of faith,"* (I Timothy 6:12), against all odds.

Let's take a final look at one example that troubles me, and should trouble the hearts of believers everywhere, as well as stir a greater challenge in all of us.

Matthew 17:14-21 states, "...Lord, have mercy on my son...And I brought him to thy disciples, and they could not cure him."

Jesus had then, and still have the Power to do what is needed. The Apostles, *after* their life-changing experiences with Jesus, had power. They were given *"Power and authority to trample upon serpents and scorpions, and [physical and mental strength and ability] over all the power that the enemy (possesses)..." (Luke 10:19 Amplified Bible),* including evident signs that *"shall follow them that believe; In My name shall they cast out devils..." (Mark 16:17)*

We, however, are not having enough life-changing experiences with the Power of Christ. *We* who are called by His Name, have been given the same power and authority. We have been Washed by the Blood. We are Fire Baptized. We are supposed to be Filled with The Holy Ghost and Speaking with New Tongues. Now, either we're not being taught properly, not being taught at all, don't have time, not available long enough for teaching, not applying it properly, have the wrong motive, wrong heart, our spirits are tainted, we're full of self, and in constant competition with other *things* or people: you pick.

Matthew 17:16 says, *"The man brought his son to the disciples and "they" could not cure him."* Not Jesus! *We* are making Jesus look bad. *We* are causing others not to believe in the *life-changing* gospel by *our* example. It is *us* giving *Him* a bad name.

Verse 19 says, "…then the disciples took Jesus aside and asked, why…?" WHY? WHY COULDN'T WE CAST THE DEMON OUT? Now, they're embarrassed and wondering why nothing is happening.

Please allow me to shed a little light and suggest a few possibilities regarding why there may not be too much response to our little *"acts of faith."* We are not **denying** ourselves enough. We are not, *on a consistent basis*, doing what it takes to walk in **purposed** power and *pre-ordained* works intended for us from the beginning. We don't come together enough. We want the power, but don't want to pay the price. We may do once a week, but please, let's not talk **DAILY**, let alone *"until midnight.*

Some may say, "Come on Pastor, it's 11:30, I **gotta** go! I have things to do. People to see. Appointments to keep!" It's sad to say, we can keep with the rigorous schedules of our day, yet have an uncanny inability to keep our hands raised for thirty minutes during praise and worship, or stand upon our feet to give reverence to God, whom *we say* we love and serve, and who *giveth us* richly all things to enjoy, according to 1 Timothy 6:17.

The people in the following scripture cried out with one voice for the space of two (2) hours to a god whose eye **could not** see, whose ear **could not** hear, nor respond in *their* time of trouble. If they could do that, how much more for us, who serve the true and living God, who can see all things…He knows all things, and who constantly hears when we cry out to Him day and night?

"But when they knew that he was a Jew, all with one voice about the space of two hours cried out, Great is Diana of the Ephesians. And when the town clerk had appeased the people, he said, Ye men of Ephesus, what man is there that knoweth not how that the city of the Ephesians is a worshipper of the great goddess Diana, and of the image which fell down from Jupiter?"
(Acts 19:34, 35)

"And Elijah came unto all the people, and said, How long halt ye between two opinions? If the Lord be God, follow him: but if Baal, then follow him. And the people answered him not a word."
(I Kings 18:21)

"And call ye on the name of your gods, and I will call on the name of the Lord: and the God that answereth by fire, let him be God. And all the people answered and said, it is well spoken. And Elijah said unto the prophets of Baal, choose you one bullock for yourselves, and dress it first; for ye are many; and call on the name of your gods,

but put no fire under. And they took the bullock which was given them, and they dressed it, and called on the name of Baal from morning even until noon, saying, O Baal, hear us. But there was no voice, nor any that answered. And they leaped upon the altar which was made. And it came to pass at noon, that Elijah mocked them, and said, Cry aloud: for he is a god; either he is talking, or he is pursuing, or he is in a journey, or peradventure he sleepeth, and must be awaked. And they cried aloud and cut themselves after their manner with knives and lancets, till the blood gushed out upon them."
(1 Kings 18: 24-28)

If this to a false god, surely what should be held back from The True and Living God NOT made by man's hands and from whom ALL blessings flow?

"But Christ being come an high priest of good things to come, by a greater and more perfect tabernacle, not made with hands, that is to say, not of this building" (Heb 9:11)

"God that made the world and all things therein, seeing that he is Lord of heaven and earth, dwelleth not in temples made with hands; Neither is worshipped with men's hands, as though he needed anything, seeing he giveth to all life, and breath, and all things." (Acts 17: 24-25)

"Thine, O Lord is the greatness, and the power, and the glory, and the victory, and the majesty: for all that is in the heaven and in the earth is Thine; Thine is the kingdom, O Lord, and Thou art exalted as head above all. Both riches and honour come of thee, and thou reignest over all; and in thine hand is power and might; and in Thine hand it is to make great, and to give strength unto all. Now therefore, our God, we thank Thee, and praise Thy glorious name. But who am I, and what is my people, that we should be able to offer so willingly after this sort? for all things come of Thee, and of Thine own have we given Thee. For we are strangers before Thee, and <u>sojourners,</u> as were all our fathers: our days on the earth are as a shadow, and there is <u>none abiding.</u> O Lord our God, all this <u>store</u> that we have prepared to build Thee an house for Thine holy name cometh of Thine hand, and is all Thine own. I know also, my God, that Thou <u>triest</u> the heart, and hast pleasure in uprightness. As for me, in the uprightness of mine heart I have willingly <u>offered</u> all these things: and now have I seen with joy Thy people, which are present here, to offer willingly unto Thee."
(1 Chronicles 29:11-17)

Who "DAILY loadeth us with benefits!" Blessed be the Lord, who daily loadeth us with benefits, even the God of our salvation. Selah."
(Psalms 68:19)

Who delivers out of all troubles! "I will bless the Lord at all times: his praise shall continually be in my mouth. My soul shall make her boast in the Lord: the humble shall hear thereof and be glad. O magnify the Lord with me and let us exalt his name together. I sought the Lord, and he heard me, and delivered me from all my fears. They looked unto him and were lightened: and their faces were not ashamed. This poor man cried, and the Lord heard him, and saved him out of all his troubles. The angel of the Lord encampeth round about them that fear him, and delivereth them. O taste and see that the Lord is good: blessed is the man that trusteth in him. O fear the Lord, ye his saints: for there is no want to them that fear him. The young lions do lack and suffer hunger: but they that seek the Lord shall not want any good thing. Come, ye children, hearken unto me: I will teach you the fear of the Lord. What man is he that desireth life, and loveth many days, that he may see good? Keep thy tongue from evil, and thy lips from speaking guile. Depart from evil, and do good; seek peace, and pursue it. The eyes of the Lord are upon the righteous, and his ears are open unto their cry. The face of the Lord is against them that do evil, to cut off the remembrance of them from the earth. The righteous cry, and the Lord heareth, and delivereth them out of all their troubles. The Lord is nigh unto them that are of a broken heart; and saveth such as be of a contrite spirit.

Many are the afflictions of the righteous: but the Lord delivereth him out of them all. He keepeth all his bones: not one of them is broken. Evil shall slay the wicked: and they that hate the righteous shall be desolate. The Lord redeemeth the soul of his servants: and none of them that trust in him shall be desolate"

Psalms 34 in its entirety, with emphasis on verses six and seventeen!

However, and rather unfortunate, is when catastrophe strikes, we run to the church *wanting, expecting* and **demanding** God to work as if He's some type of magician and His works are some form of magic. We try to *buy* our healing and *pay* the way for our miracles. WARNING…may I remind you of the last few fellows who thought the true power and blessings of God could be bought with money or deceptive maneuvers?

"And when Simon saw that through laying on of the apostles' hands the Holy Ghost was given, he offered them money, saying, 'Give me also this power, that on whomsoever I lay hands, he may receive the Holy Ghost.' But Peter said unto him, Thy money perish with thee, because thou hast thought that the gift of God may be purchased with money. Thou hast neither part nor lot in this matter: for thy heart is not right in the sight of God. Repent therefore of this thy wickedness, and pray God, if perhaps the thought

of thine heart may be forgiven thee. For I perceive that thou art in the gall of bitterness, and in the bond of iniquity. Then answered Simon, and said, 'Pray ye to the Lord for me, that none of these things which ye have spoken come upon me.'" (Acts 8:19, 20-24)

"But a certain man named Ananias with his wife Sapphira sold a piece of property, And with his wife's knowledge and connivance he kept back and wrongfully appropriated some of the proceeds, bringing only a part and putting it at the feet of the apostles. But Peter said, Ananias, why has Satan filled your heart that you should lie to and attempt to deceive the Holy Spirit, and should [in violation of your promise] withdraw secretly and appropriate to your own use part of the price from the sale of the land? As long as it remained unsold, was it not still your own? And [even] after it was sold, was not [the money] at your disposal and under your control? Why then, is it that you have proposed and purposed in your heart to do this thing? [How could you have the heart to do such a deed?] You have not [simply] lied to men [playing false and showing yourself utterly deceitful] but to God. Upon hearing these words, Ananias fell down and died. And great dread and terror took possession of all who heard of it. And the young men arose and wrapped up [the body] and carried it out and buried it. Now after an interval of

*about three hours his wife came in, not having
learned of what had happened. And Peter said to
her, Tell me, did you sell the land for so much?
Yes, she said, for so much. Then Peter said to
her, How could you two have agreed and
conspired together to try to deceive the Spirit of
the Lord? Listen! The feet of those who have
buried your husband are at the door, and they
will carry you out [also]."*
Acts 5: 1-9 (Amplified Bible)

We expect God to show up for us at *our* beck and
call, as though some great fate is *owed* or *due* us.
We expect Him to come upon our terms and *only*
under our conditions, can this mighty act or deed
be so, else we label Him and count Him among
false gods and mere man.

I guarantee if we would just ask the Lord to *"have
mercy on us,"* as did the Father regarding his son
in the book of Matthew, He would meet us right
where we are. The man with the unclean spirit, as
discussed in the book of Mark, had been *"crying
and cutting himself... always, night and day!"*
Likewise, many of us have been crying in various
ways, **looking for a way out**. What we fail to
realize is that there is a side to each of us that
desire and want to be *totally* free. There is yet a
part that is often bound by the systems and dictates
of this life and world in which we live.
Nevertheless, if we would cry out, **He will** hear
and deliver. Let's not waste another minute!

Run to Him and watch Jesus speak to every circumstance, every situation, and **command** every unclean thing in and around to **come out** in order that we, too, may be whole and found in our "*right*" mind, according to Mark 5:15. With everything we're facing, and *seemingly* no solution in sight, I would say we need more *intimate* contact with The Master, and *evident* power that we've been with Him.

"And he ordained twelve, that they should be with him, and that he might send them forth to preach" (Mk. 3:14); "Now when they saw the boldness of Peter and John, and perceived that they were unlearned and ignorant men, they marvelled; and they took knowledge of them, that they had been with Jesus." (Acts 4:13)

It's evident we have money. It's also an evident sign in scripture, as well as urgent matters of today, what money attempted to buy and could not. No price can *buy* deliverance. No price can *buy* the solution to the problems we face on a day to day basis. No price can *buy* inner peace…the Peace that passes all understanding…The times, you couldn't explain *how* you've made it this far… the times, you didn't know *why* it was someone else, and you were not dead…the times you *knew* it should've been you. However, you're still here.

Now, we're living in a time where death has accompanied much sickness. I may add, no amount of money has been able to stop sickness and disease from taking countless lives of loved ones from amongst us all. Beloved, let's be about the Father's business, trusting He will take care of ours and balance out the rest! Be encouraged. You have nothing to *lose*, yet so much to *gain*! Remember, the whole world is waiting, as stated in Romans 8.

*…What are you **losing** of value in order to **gain**?*

*…What has you "**selling out**" at the sake of your soul?*

*…What **so called** securities have you trusted your soul to?*

BARELY A RICH MAN

Throughout scripture, there are evidenced results of how much more POWER has made the difference in various situations as opposed to natural resources.

Galatians 6:1 conveys, "Brethren, if a man be overtaken in a fault, ye which are spiritual, restore such an one in the spirit of meekness; considering thyself, lest thou also be tempted."

"We then that are strong ought to bear the infirmities of the weak, and not to please ourselves." Romans 15:1

It does not say, "*ye who are rich.*" There is constant instruction for those who are rich in faith, rather than finances, to make a difference in one's life based on their measure of faith in the word of God at work in them. As a matter of fact, the scripture that is often referenced regarding the "*rich young ruler*" in Luke shows us how he found himself faced with the challenge of making a choice between his *natural* riches and his very *soul*s' salvation in God. The end result clearly states how he walked away, not only ***sorrowful***, but ***very sorrowful***, for he was **very** rich.

*"And a certain ruler asked him, saying, Good Master, what shall I do to inherit eternal life? And Jesus said unto him, Why callest thou Me good? none is good, save One, that is, God. Thou knowest the commandments, Do not commit adultery, Do not kill, Do not steal, Do not bear false witness, Honour thy father and thy mother. And he said, All these have I kept from my youth up. Now when Jesus heard these things, he said unto him, Yet lackest thou one thing: sell all that thou hast, and distribute unto the poor, and thou shalt have treasure in heaven: and come, follow Me. And when he heard this, he was very <u>sorrowful</u>: for he was very rich. And when Jesus saw that he was very <u>sorrowful</u>, He said, How hardly shall they that have riches enter into the kingdom of God! For it is easier for a camel to go through a needle's eye, than for a rich man to enter into the kingdom of God. And they that heard it said, Who then can be saved? And he said, The things which are impossible with men are possible with God. Then Peter said, Lo, we have left all, and followed thee. And he said unto them, <u>Verily</u> I say unto you, There is no man that hath left house, or parents, or brethren, or wife, or children, for the kingdom of God's sake, Who shall not receive <u>manifold</u> more in this present time, and in the world to come life everlasting."
(Luke 18:18-30)*

Equal to the response of the young ruler, I find it heartbreaking that one would choose *stuff*, which can be replaced, over a life far more valuable and irreplaceable. I'm sure it breaks the heart of the Father to see us turn away from all that He has given, and made available to us, in order to choose not only those *things* which will fade away, but that which will, *in the end*, come to naught.

"Lay not up for yourselves treasures upon earth, where moth and rust doth corrupt, and where thieves break through and steal: But lay up for yourselves treasures in heaven, where neither moth nor rust doth corrupt, and where thieves do not break through nor steal: For where your treasure is, there will your heart be also."
(Matthew 6:19-21)

"For in one hour so great riches is come to nought. And every shipmaster, and all the company in ships, and sailors, and as many as trade by sea, stood afar off." (Revelation 18:17)

In verses 7, 13 and 14 of Revelation, Chapter 18, the word *"All"* symbolizes how riches in various ways have affected us. *"How much she hath glorified herself, and lived deliciously, so much torment and sorrow give her: for she saith in her heart, I sit a queen, and am no widow, and shall see no sorrow; And cinnamon, and odours, and ointments, and frankincense, and wine, and oil, and fine flour, and wheat, and beasts, and sheep, and horses, and chariots, and slaves, and souls of men. And the fruits that thy soul lusted after are departed from thee, and all things which were dainty and goodly are departed from thee, and thou shalt find them no more at all."*

Additional scripture supports how riches have turned hearts, caused individuals to err off the path of intended purpose, and have destroyed many great men and women of God, both naturally and spiritually.

Luke chapter18, verse 24 says, "And when Jesus saw that he was very sorrowful, he said, How hardly shall they that have riches enter into the kingdom of God!"

Another version in Mark 10:23, 24 says, *"And Jesus looked round about, and saith unto His disciples, How hardly shall they that have riches enter into the kingdom of God! And the disciples were astonished at His words. But Jesus answereth again, and saith unto them, Children, how hard is it for them that trust in riches to enter into the kingdom of God!"*

As we continue in Luke, Chapter 18, verse 25 says, *"For it is easier for a camel to go through a needle's eye, than for a rich man to enter into the kingdom of God." And they that heard it said, WHO THEN CAN BE SAVED?"*

Notice the question. They **did not** ask, "Who then can **enter** in?" Their concern **was not** making it in; their concern **was** *being saved – with riches*. The disciples almost gave an analogy suggesting the *impossibility* of *having money* and *being saved*. Their statement, "Who then...?" made it obvious that there were **several** *saved, rich* individuals, *including themselves*. So, the scripture... *"For it is easier... than for a rich man,"* caused them **great concern**. Even as it did the rich young ruler, it would suggest to many, if left with the **choice** regarding salvation or riches, forget this salvation thing, *take the money and run*!

The question then becomes not *who can be saved*, but who can have **all** this, **be** saved, **stay** saved and **not allow** it to affect them? The answer is found in verse 27 of the same Chapter of Luke, *"And He said, "The things which are impossible with men are possible with God."*

Again, *"With men it is impossible, but not with God: for with God all things are possible." (Mark 10:27)"*

71

God's concern is **not** *you having riches*; God's concern **is** *riches having you*! This definitely should clear up the question, "Does God desire me to be rich?" *"**Beloved, I wish above all things that thou mayest prosper..".** (3 John 1:2)* The sole purpose of God desiring us to prosper is in order to advance the Kingdom of God.

The point of forsaking all and following Him is to see to what you are more attached. *"And when they had brought their ships to land, they forsook all, and followed him" (Luke. 5:11). "And he said unto them, "Verily I say unto you, There is no man that hath left house, or parents, or brethren, or wife, or children, for the kingdom of God's sake, Who shall not receive manifold more in this present time, and in the world to come life everlasting." (Luke 18:29-30)*

The reason He wants us to have more in this life is for *His covenant* to be established in the earth, not our *own* agendas or our *ideas* of what that establishment looks like. *"But thou shalt remember the Lord thy God: for it is he that giveth thee power to get wealth, that he may establish his covenant which he sware unto thy fathers, as it is this day" (Deuteronomy 8:18)*

Neither this book nor the word of God was written to come against riches, prosperity or wealth. It is evident in verse 26 as stated before, that the disciples were rich, but obviously worried. This book is however, written to prayerfully put all things back into their proper perspectives so we *can* live life and *that* (life) **more abundantly,** the way He intended… *"Pleasing, being fruitful unto every good work… (Colossians 1:10)* to the glory of God the Father. And truly *good works* for the Kingdom takes *good money*!

In Luke 18:29, 30, it is evident that God **is not** trying to *take, nor keep,* anything from us. He is, however, trying to make sure nothing separates us from Him, nor becomes more important than what *He intended* in His *original* plan and purpose (**origin**: beginning; starting point).

Let's visit Genesis 1:26-28…It conveys, *"Be fruitful, and multiply, and replenish the earth, and subdue it: and have DOMINION."* We become fruitful, begin multiplying (in more ways than one). Then, we find ourselves, at some point, *self*-serving, *self*-centered and unfortunately, rather conscious or unconscious, we lose sight of our purpose of origin in the earth. Then, we end up *thrown* in a direction that was never intended from the beginning.

God wants *us* in control. He doesn't want *things* in control of us! He wants to be assured that if He *asks anything* of what **He has given** us steward over, there would be no hesitation or fear of loss. Rather, He desires faith towards Him as **our source** *of all things*. After all, everything belongs to Him. Yet, they are placed in our hands *only* to determine how well we handle the management thereof.

People desire to be *"fat"* in their bank accounts, *fat* in their businesses, *fat* in their ministries, and *fat* in their overall endeavors of life. Yet, they fail to search the scriptures concerning God's desire for us to be *made fat,* pointing in the direction of **true** *riches*!

Luke 16:11 says*... **"If therefore ye have not been faithful in the unrighteous mammon** [money]**, who will commit to your trust the true riches?"***

Proverbs 28:25 says... "but he that putteth his trust in the Lord shall be made fat."

Fat: H1878 dasen, to thrive, grow fat; to anoint, give health; to prosper, be satisfied, be soaked (with fat); to be covered with fat: -made fat, waxen fat.

God's desire for us to be *made fat* is to be *soaked* in His anointing, *covered* with *His ability* to remove burdens and destroy yokes! The power to thrive in health, be satisfied, and *made fat* spiritually and financially *is* in His plan for us and obtainable, *if* we determine to do it *His way*.

Over the years, I've heard I Timothy 6:5 *partially* quoted and although with excitement, equally with the misinterpretation **"...that gain is godliness."** However, when completely stated and properly applied, it reads...**"Perverse disputing of men of corrupt minds, and destitute of the truth, supposing that gain is godliness: from such withdraw thyself."** It goes on to say, **"But godliness with contentment is great gain. For we brought nothing into this world, and it is certain we can carry nothing out. And having food and raiment let us be therewith content. But they that will be rich fall into temptation and a snare, and into many foolish and hurtful lusts, which drown men in destruction and perdition. For the love of money is the root of all evil: which while some coveted after, they have erred from the faith, and pierced themselves through with many sorrows."**

In verse 17 of I Timothy, it goes on to say, **"Charge them that are rich in this world, that they be not high-minded, nor trust in uncertain riches, but in the living God, who giveth us richly all things to enjoy; that they do good, that they be** *rich in good works, ready to distribute, willing to communicate; Laying up in store for themselves a good foundation against the time to come, that they may lay hold on eternal life."*

More than ever, I pray that we stop simply quoting the word and begin *"rightly dividing the word of truth,"* instead of working the word for our own self gain and benefit.

"Study to shew thyself approved unto God, a workman that needeth not to be ashamed, rightly dividing the word of truth." (2Timothy 2:15)

I pray that we become *fat* in the word of God, in The Spirit of The Living God, in the truth about "what is written about our God, our life *"in Him"* and the *"Zoe"* (life) of Christ *in us*!

I pray that we become *fat* in order that we may **gain** the excellency of the **knowledge** of Christ Jesus our Lord.

"Yea doubtless, and I count all things but loss for the excellency of the knowledge of Christ Jesus my Lord: for whom I have suffered the loss of all things, and do count them but dung, that I may win Christ." (Philippians 3:8)

Becoming *spiritually fat* places a weight of **wealth** *within* which no bank could ever hold and nothing and no one can take away. Nowhere in scripture do we see money performing the works or being exchanged for the power and miracles wrought by the hands of the apostles. The works, mind you, which made all the difference in the lives of countless individuals throughout scripture. That kind of Wealth worked, because of what was *"in"* them, not because of what they had *"on"* them. Remember Simon, ***"Thy money perish with thee...thou hast neither part nor lot in this matter: for thy heart is not right in the sight of God."***

Wealth to change lives!
Wealth to transform!

With the state that the world is in today, I'd say we would be better off with *this kind* of wealth being made available instead of *"talk"* of more money. Interestingly enough, the more we talk of money, ironically, the more of a financial deficit in which we seem to find ourselves. Yes, money has its place and contrary to belief, there is no shortage of it. On the other hand, with the number of incoming conferences and outgoing messages, there is, however, a shortage of POWER available to combat the growing number of problems we face on a daily basis.

As we read, not only in the book of Acts, but throughout Jesus' ministry, it is clearly indicated evident change in the lives of people, through the power of God, by Jesus Himself and the Apostles. Several examples were given previously. Nonetheless, let us visit the example of the impotent man at the gate called *"Beautiful."* For starters, how can we associate *anything* in our lives with *"beautiful,"* when several things *within* and *about* us are **"bowed down," "bent over," "curled up," "lame,"** and **"disfigured?"**

People of God, let's paint a clear picture here. This man was *carried*...and laid at the Gate called *"Beautiful"* daily, *"And a certain man lame from his mother's womb was carried, whom they laid daily at the gate of the temple which is called Beautiful, to ask alms of them that entered into the temple." (Acts 3:2)*

He was **carried** to the temple - the house of God - the church - and *laid* there *daily*. He was carried without any expectation, obviously, from those carrying him, those entering in, or him. They were merely *satisfied* with a little **change** (coined money), rather than actual **change** (life transformation). How beautiful is that?

This impotent man, like many in life, as well as in the Body of Christ, was being looked over by those who go into the temple every day. People were going and coming, doing the normal thing of *their* customs...entering the temple (**to pray**), leaving, and going on about *their* business. In this situation, how *normal* was it to carry him to the gate everyday and drop him **outside**? Why not at least take him *into* the temple while prayer is going on, peradventure, in the midst of sitting there some miracle may befall him?

Perhaps, like many of us and many a situation like it, we tend to give individuals only what can temporarily bring relief in order to ensure there's not too much of a demand placed on us. Perhaps, the individual only wants what's easy, so as not to have a responsibility to anything.

Was there no one interested in the true transformation for the impotent man?

Is there anyone at all interested in true transformation for the impotent conditions of this life?

How often do we proceed pass situations into the sanctuary, *masking* the *true* need with a temporary fix? Have the *norms* of Sundays' services, conferences, retreats, revivals, convocations, and gatherings of the sort, **deadened**, **desensitized** and **numbed** our sensitivity to one another? Has it dulled us to the *reality* of what's really needed, what's been made available and the sacrifice it really takes to make and see a difference? Or, have we so long seen *too little* works amongst us that we've *settled* for the *little* **change** (our conditions), and have become satisfied with being *carried*?

How beautiful is that to go day after day **into prayer**, *supposedly* into the **very presence** of an **ALMIGHTY** God, barely expecting to receive for your situation, let alone dare to believe to receive for another? How long will we continue in a *"form"* of godliness, yet denying the power thereof? ***"Having a form of godliness but denying the power thereof: from such turn away." (2 Timothy 3:5)***

We're denying the truth of need all around us. We're denying the need for *true change (not chump change)*! We need a change of mind, a change of heart, a change of ways! Just a change! What are we really praying about? What are we really praying for? Why are we petitioning a Throne of Grace to obtain mercy and find grace to

80

help in time of need if we're not *expecting* to see or experience what we went in for?

> *"Let us therefore come boldly unto the throne of grace, that we may obtain mercy, and find grace to help in time of need."*
> *(Hebrews 4:16)*

> *"And when he had considered the thing, he came to the house of Mary the mother of John, whose surname was Mark; where many were gathered together praying. And as Peter knocked at the door of the gate, a damsel came to hearken, named Rhoda. And when she knew Peter's voice, she opened not the gate for gladness, but ran in, and told how Peter stood before the gate. And they said unto her, Thou art mad. But she constantly affirmed that it was even so. Then said they, It is his angel. But Peter continued knocking: and when they had opened the door, and saw him, they were astonished."*
> *(Acts 12:12-16)*

Where are the "Peters" and "Johns" who will *fasten* their eyes and see a thing for what it is, call that thing out and be done with it? Where are the *friends* who will *carry* upon their shoulders the impotent of life, tear the roofs off and get down and dirty in order to **refuse** to see individuals remain in the conditions they've been lying in for years?

Where are the Believers who *go in* to prayer *"with all boldness,"* praying… *"By stretching forth Thine hand to heal; and that signs and wonders may be done by the name of Thy holy child Jesus, then come out of prayer having the place shaken where they are assembled?" (Acts 4:29-31)*

How do you think the previously stated behavior made the impotent man feel? Although he was *carried*, he was not discounted in the eyes of God. Therefore, and it cannot be denied, the possible *tainted view* he more than likely had regarding *"church people."* Likewise, how do you think it makes people feel everyday, who frequent in and out of churches all over the globe? There are individuals who are stepped over, passed by, and made to feel their problems aren't important enough. Oftentimes, it is due to the *social customs* arising in our sanctuaries, and the increasing growth of politics associated within our assemblies. *The church is losing its place, its voice and its respect by virtue of the lack of having what it takes to do what is needed.*

The Apostles, **in the midst** of their *flaws, failures* and *imperfections*, paid the price, and overcame astonishing challenges. They operated in the realm of the miraculous and became eyewitnesses to the life-changing gospel of Jesus Christ, *as a normal part of life.*

"Now, when they had passed through Amphipolis and Apollonia, they came to Thessalonica, where was a synagogue of the Jews: And Paul, as his manner was, went in unto them, and three sabbath days reasoned with them out of the scriptures, Opening and alleging, that Christ must needs have suffered, and risen again from the dead; and that this Jesus, whom I preach unto you, is Christ. And some of them believed and consorted with Paul and Silas; and of the devout Greeks a great multitude, and of the chief women not a few. But the Jews which believed not, moved with envy, took unto them certain lewd fellows of the baser sort, and gathered a company, and set all the city on an uproar, and assaulted the house of Jason, and sought to bring them out to the people. And when they found them not, they drew Jason and certain brethren unto the rulers of the city, crying, these that have turned the world upside down are come hither also." (Acts 17:1-6)

Including the lives of everyone they encountered, they counted it an honor and a privilege to be persecuted for Christ's sake. Once they experienced a level of *"being with Him,"* and moving in a POWER undeniable, nothing else mattered!

We are losing battles every day as it relates to children, family structure, marriage and impactful ministries - to the world and its competitive edge of music, television, video and various forms of what's labeled as *"entertainment."* As the Apostles moved in power, people were added to the church daily. People are not being added in the sense of the *acts* of the Apostles. It's more so, in the sense of *revolving* amongst churches, when there is enough souls out there to fill every church on every corner – which, by the way, is another disgrace to the Body of Christ. Nevertheless, it's better to have a church than a liquor store, if that helps somebody to feel better.

Something *is not* right. As it is written… ***"Money answereth all things…"*** But Money *is not* "**The**" Answer. I could almost guarantee, if we **got into the lives of people** *with* **"***change***"** (the right kind), we would have no problem **getting into the pockets of people** *for change*. There is so much more to be received than what we have gone after in the past. So, for everyone out there who's getting as nervous as the rich young ruler…*relax.* There is **NOTHING** you can give up **for God** and not have it returned to you one hundred-fold!

Luke 18:29, 30 says, "And he said unto them, Verily I say unto you, There is no man that hath left house, or parents, or brethren, or wife, or children, for the kingdom of God's sake, Who shall not receive manifold more in this present time, and in the world to come life everlasting."

God is trying to get it to us right now, not in the *by and by*. However, it **must** be done His way. The word *"Manifold"* consists of many times over (mucho grande)! Manifold is much more than we can think or perceive. It connotes a much larger scale than what our minds can comprehend. This present time consists of the time we are in **now**. Understanding Him, means we understand His principle: Prosperity *is* His will! You're actually *not giving up* anything. Rather, you're *gaining* everything.

I **challenge** each of us to leave the former things and come into a greater place of prosperity for which everyone can acknowledge is a need. I **charge** us to get into the God who truly has come *"that we might have life,"* in more ways than we can imagine.

"The thief cometh not, but for to steal, and to kill, and to destroy: I am come that they might have life, and that they might have it more abundantly." (John 10:10)

*...Choose ye this day...What will **your** choice be?*

LIFE...

AND THAT MORE ABUNDANTLY

I recall a moment on the altar, as a sister in Christ and I shared. She began to speak out of her love and appreciation to our God, yet all at once, with tears streaming from her eyes, she fervently belted, "I ain't got nothing!" "What are you saying?" I exclaimed back as the Spirit of the Lord began to unction me in the way of comfort, edification and exhortation. "You have everything!" As the Holy Spirit continued upon me, He enlightened me to share concerning our outlook on what *we define* as nothing. We have *countless* opportunities to connect with the wisdom, knowledge, revelation and word that surrounds us via the saints. However, in order for it to be *released* to us, whatever it may be, we think we have need of, most of us stay too *closed* within our own selves and people groups. Sometimes, we *refuse* to make known or share what we have. We, then, miss recognizing that *"life more abundantly"* is right at our fingertips.

She had a beautiful family and a loving and supporting husband, who likewise adored God. She, however, like many of us, hadn't tapped into the **wealth of resources** made available to her and the **bounty of riches** *within* her to bring to her those *"tangible"* things *she felt* to be missing in her life.

We discussed in an earlier chapter how without proper guidance and nurturing many individuals *within* and *without* the Body, go with a wealth of riches and resources **untapped**...*Never* making *"full proof of their ministries," never* **discharging all duties**, n*ever* reaching their fullest potential.

In other words, there are countless individuals who may never even begin tapping into the gifts, talents, and abilities given them. Thus, never experiencing life, and *that* more abundantly. However, these individuals do love and serve God with their whole heart. The tragedy in all this is failure to recognize, more than anything, that we have been given the greatest gift one could ever possess in the greatest value one could ever place a price on... *"Christ in us*, the hope of glory!"

And while *that hope* and *level of glory* remains untapped due to time **not spent** in His presence, in fellowship and sweet communion with Him, His word and the assembling of ourselves together with the saints, The **King of Glory awaits** that time with us. In order to show us what it is He has placed on the inside of us, we must learn *how* to tap into and bring about every resource available - through spending time with Him - who is our source, our way and our life.

"In Him was [and is] life; and the life was the light of men" (St. John 1:4)

"I AM the Way, the Truth and the Life." (St. John 14:6

"If ye abide [to take up residence; to live in; to dwell permanently] in Me, and my words abide in you, ye shall ask what ye will, and it shall be done unto you." (St. John 15:7)

"I AM the True vine...Abide in Me...As the branch cannot bear fruit of itself, except it abide in the vine; now more can ye, except ye abide in Me...for without Me ye can do NOTHING." (St. John 15:1, 4, 5)

Now, if we can do "*nothing*" without Him, what makes us think we can accumulate "*something*" without Him that will remain and have any type of substance to it?

Again, Deuteronomy 8:18 reminds us that it is God that gives us the **power** to get wealth that He may establish **His covenant**. He seeks to hold NOTHING back from us as He desires only to give us EVERYTHING!

"He that spared not his own Son, but delivered him up for us all, how shall he not with him also freely give us all things?" (Romans 8:32)

When we begin to realize that Jesus *is* our way to prosperity, purpose and *true riches*, then will we cease from our own works, trying to accomplish what we, in and of ourselves are unable to do. In Him, there is life. In His presence, there is peace. In His presence, there is "*fullness.*" Everything needed to "*live life*," "*give life*," and "*be life*" to many areas of death, darkness and disease all around us.

"Thou wilt shew me the path of life: in thy presence is fulness of joy; at thy right hand there are pleasures for evermore." (Psalms 16:11)

We have everything needed to **preach** Good News to the poor; to **heal** the broken-hearted and to **announce** that the captives shall be released and the blind shall see, that the downtrodden shall be freed from their oppressors, and that **God is ready** to give blessings to all who come to Him.

"The Spirit of the Lord is upon me; he has appointed me to preach Good News to the poor; he has sent me to heal the brokenhearted and to announce that captives shall be released and the blind shall see, that the downtrodden shall be freed from their oppressors, and that God is ready to give blessings to all who come to him."
(Luke 4:18-19 The Living Bible)

"Christ in us, the hope of Glory: To whom God would make known what is the riches of the glory of this mystery among the Gentiles; which is Christ in you, the hope of glory."
(Colossians 1:27)

The Creator of not only *"what's"* being made, but *"who's"* being made. I cannot stress enough everything we need *is* on the inside of us. Everything we need *is* in Him!

Luke 12:15 says, "And He said unto them, Take heed, and beware of covetousness: for a man's life consisteth not in the abundance of the things which he possesseth." (KJV)

"Beware! Don't always be wishing for what you don't have. For real life and real living are not related to how rich we are." (TLB)

Then he said, "Beware! Guard against every kind of greed. Life is not measured by how much you own." (New Living Translation)

Then Jesus said to them all, "Watch yourselves! Keep from wanting all kinds of things you should not have. A man's life is not made up of things, even if he has many riches." (New Life Bible)

Then he said to them, "Watch out! Be on your guard against all kinds of greed; life does not consist in an abundance of possessions." (NIV)

Speaking to the people, he went on, "Take care! Protect yourself against the least bit of greed. Life is not defined by what you have, even when you have a lot." (The Message Bible)

And He said to them, "Guard yourselves and keep free from all covetousness (the immoderate desire for wealth, the greedy longing to have more); for a man's life does not consist in and is not derived from possessing overflowing abundance or that which is over and above his needs." (Amplified Bible)

I listed a variety to paint a *clear picture* of the thought patterns of what *does not* rank top priority with God as it relates to wealth and the value of what a man's life *does not* consist of based solely upon *our definition* of life. I would dare to say that a man's life *does* consist of the abundance of awareness one has to the knowledge of his Creator. For what a man *"does not know"* can hurt, and what a man possesses, if wrongfully used cannot only hurt him, but everyone around that is affected by the mismanagement and misuse of those possessions or power.

Unfortunately, since there is not an abundance of awareness towards the knowledge of Him from whom all things consist and was made, there has not been an abundance of examples of *how* to activate the life of God, in light of demonstrating that life while in *this world*, but not of it. If there is no understanding of *what* you house, and *why* you've been given what it is you have, you are left unaware of how to *properly* operate, as you move forward in a false sense of security.

Equally dangerous to one who does not know the purpose as to *why* they have been placed on this earth, is one of an inexperienced jet pilot flyer. Though the *aircraft* is **full** and **appears** ready, if not *properly* piloted to **direct the aircraft's course**, there is no knowledge on *how* to get where you need to go. Thus, buttons are tampered with that were never intended to be touched, and things done towards the mishandling of that aircraft that disrupts its initial purpose. This problem leaves much room for some form of disaster to it, and all those involved.

We **must** be trained on so many levels and brought to several areas of maturation concerning what has been given us. This ensures its proper use for the purpose in which God originally intended.

Let's make a conscious decision to know what has been made accessible to us through the life, death burial and resurrection of our Lord and Savior, Jesus Christ. For many of us, making this decision will bring struggle and a war within ourselves. This war will stem from a roller coaster of emotion, challenge and fear. For some, it will be the refusal to move from the comfort of what we've been accustomed to for so long. For others, it will be the concern for what peers, people and loved ones will think.

I'm reminded of a passage in scripture where God came to Moses to inform him of what He wanted Moses to do. *Exodus 3:10, "Come now, therefore, and I will send you…that you may bring my people…out…And Moses said to God, who am I, that I should go…?"*

Let me pause right here and say, God knew before you what you were all about, what you would be doing, will do and have done, so stop it! THERE IS NOTHING NEITHER YOU NOR I COULD DO TO MERIT GOD'S CHOICE OF USING US. It's simply because He just CHOOSES to use us!

"And Moses said unto God, "Behold, when I come unto the children…and shall say unto them. You have sent me, and they shall say to me, what is His Name? what shall I say unto them?"

Let's relate this to our day and time. Imagine, God coming to any one of us right where we are. He begins to inform us of what it was He wanted us to do, after years of doing things according to the way we've been accustomed to doing it or the way we *perceived* it to be correct.

> ***Proverbs 14:12 says, "There is a way which seemeth right..."*** *[and that way it may very well bring success, but is it the success God intended for you? Is it the way He intended it to be? Is it His way?]*

> ***Joshua 1:8 says, "That you may observe to do all that is written in it. For then you will make your way prosperous, and then you will have good success."***

I think it's safe to say God doesn't mind us making our way prosperous, however, by what method we obtain the success and the type of success does matter to Him.

Ladies and gentlemen, brothers and sisters, there seems to be a great deal of honor being given to the *name* [God]. They do this, in light of one's success, particularly in the music and entertainment industry, perhaps without adequate knowledge of thus said God.

According to Moses, the people asked what the *name* of which Moses was coming in and claiming to represent. Not even someone as close to God as Moses, was sure as to what *nature* and *character* of God's name *to present* to them. Likewise, according to *the way* things are being exploited and the *acts* of so many individuals, how can one believe they are giving honor to the name [God] when the very *nature* they present is contrary to the *character* of the name [God], whom I know and serve?

My question then becomes, *in what name* or *who's nature*, or in light of whose character is honor really being given? What god(s) is a person actually referring to and who is it that people are presenting? After all, the demons *say* the name and tremble!

"Thou believest that there is one God; thou doest well: the devils also believe, and tremble."
(James 2:19)

The very *name* GOD is universal in all languages, so it's not just the name; it's the person inclusive of the character and nature. So, as it relates to the *person* of the True and Living God, in the *person* of Jesus Christ, have we attached ourselves to Him so much so that we reflect His image? What we present, does it cause a reverential respect and bring about such a presence that it causes one to rid, or *consider* ridding everything impure, unwholesome, evil, unrighteous or immorally incorrect?

We are still talking about *"Life, and that more abundantly."* Nonetheless, we cannot talk about nor have this life without talking about *His* life. When we talk about the life of a person, we must touch on personality, character traits and morals. If we look at the example of *natural parents*, and we **in truth** *represent them*, most would agree there are things we would **never** be found doing. Because, we dare not associate certain behavior to them, as our life is supposed to be a **reflection** of their life. Which, in turn, would only bring embarrassment and *contradiction* to the name, the person and what was initially taught.

How, then, is there so much obscene behavior among so many today? Yet, we choose to *associate* it and make it a *reflection* of a God, who is not only HOLY, but further make it acceptable against everything He opposes and instructs us to do?

A conscious decision of continuing in a way which seems right after having received correct instruction is not only dangerous, but a direction in self destruction.

> **Hosea 4:6 says, "My people are destroyed for lack of knowledge. Because you have rejected knowledge..."**

You *put off* everything that is of God. You take prayer out of the schools. You eliminate God out of the equation, amidst a society whose principles and morals were founded on the very foundation of Christian values. Then, you invite the very consequences of the social chaos and destruction we see eating away, as does a canker worm, at what was once considered the structural pillars of our day.

Again, **Proverbs 14:12 says, "There is a way which seemeth right unto a man, but the end thereof are the ways of death."** The conclusion of *our way*, as seen in today's society, has obviously not been the answer, nor has it brought about the results needed to experience life, let alone a more abundant one.

Remember our friend the rich young ruler in Mark 10:17-30? I want to focus our attention on the latter portion of verse 17, which says, *"What shall I do that I may inherit eternal life?"* Verse 19 gives Jesus' response which says, "You know the commandments: *"Do not commit adultery,"* [well that knocks most of us out!]; *"Do not murder,"* [yet with the tongue we kill daily!].

James 3:2 reminds us, *"For we all often stumble and fall and offend in many things. And if anyone does not offend in speech [never says the wrong things], he is a fully developed character and a perfect man, able to control his whole body and to curb his entire nature." (Amplified Bible)*

As we read on in James (King James Version), it tells how literal bodies of animals and ships can be turned about and tamed by objects which appear to be very small yet hold great significance to the things mentioned.

Even so, verse 5 says, "the tongue is a little member and boasts great things, See how great a forest a little fire kindles! And the tongue is a fire, a world of iniquity: so is the tongue among our members, that it defileth the whole body, and sets on fire the course of nature; and it is set on fire of hell. For every kind of beast...is tamed and has been tamed...But no man can tame the tongue. It is an unruly evil, full of deadly poison."

In other words, a small fire can destroy an entire forest. However, something as small as the tongue, with how we speak to one another and the things we allow to come out of our mouths, can kill character, self esteem and the entire image of a person in a matter of minutes. Yes, we're still talking about *Life and that More Abundantly*.

We have so far to go with so little time to get there!

Let's return to Mark 10:19, which states, ***"Do not steal...Honor thy father and mother."*** Now skipping around, verse 21 says, ***"Then Jesus looking at him, loved him..."*** Those two particular words struck my attention immediately as the Holy Spirit revealed to me how Jesus must have felt *loving him*. Yet, he was unable to do anything regarding the ***choice*** he was about to make. Even as Jesus was affected, we too, can look at friends and family members, while loving them, be unable to do anything to stop them from the choices they are about to make. The things they are about to do or have done, will not only affect us, but cost them dearly. So, no matter how hard it may be on us at times, as Jesus does, we can only look, love and continue to pray for them. After all, **it is a choice**. Jesus knew the choice he was about to make.

The rich young ruler was doing all the right things seemingly, in his mind, for he said in verse 20, *"All these things I have kept from my youth."* These were "his" standards of how he saw to keep the laws of God.

Likewise, we flatter ourselves every Sunday in religious exercises trying to keep the laws of God, instead of trying to learn the ways of The Lord. Therefore, we leave lacking the one thing we're to walk in daily that Jesus mentioned to the ruler. It all goes back to love. In reality, everything done is done for the benefit of someone else when we choose to lose our own self interest to gain the greater value in life. You see, *living life* more abundantly involves more than just you, my friend. This is where we tend to get sidetracked and become consumed with self. Life more abundantly includes the wealth of seeing *others' lives changed and made whole*. Making the difference or a *"mark,"* as one would say, in various ways.

There is so much to be said regarding this as it relates to our lives today. If some were more concerned about their *soul* salvation and what God thinks regarding them, they would be less concerned with the views and opinions of others.

Only then, could they boldly, and with confidence, join the innumerable number of men and women of God everywhere who continue to walk into the purpose and plan God intends for our lives. Thereby, pleasing Him in every way, rather, at every turn, trying to please man!

With the increasing number of loss to morality, value and respect, one can note it has actually been that *way of life*, over time, which has caused many to compromise, minimize and even allow loss in the various *forms* and *ways* to occur. Society has become "dog eat dog, having ignored the compassion placed, for purpose, within all of us. Looking out only for ourselves has never been the original thought of God towards us. That type of mindset has only brought about all the evils we see manifested amongst us and being encountered on a day to day basis.

If God **so loved** the world that **He gave**, wouldn't it be safe to say that He desires to see that same love duplicated and exemplified in us towards one another? But we've hurt for so long and have inflicted so much pain, until the questions become, how do we come up from it all? How do we turn for the better? How do we go in the way that is right? What do we do? What do we say? Where do we start? What is the medium to bring us all to *The Way* **that is right**?

Although it will take a willingness on our part, thanks be unto God who *always* in all things cause us to triumph (in Christ Jesus). And one starting point is always sure...*"If My people, which are called by My Name, shall humble themselves, and pray, and seek My face, and turn from their wicked ways; then will I hear from Heaven, and will forgive their sin, and will heal their land."* *(2 Chronicles 7:14)*

God has nothing to do with the wickedness in the land that has swept our nation. But, thank God, there is a remedy! Let's stop misinterpreting the matter by blaming Him and start taking our rightful place, as lights, as cities, as representatives in the earth and do something. If it must start somewhere, it must start with us.

People of God, any and everyone who may be embracing the words of this book, if recalled, the rich young ruler was sad at Jesus' words and went away very sorrowful, for he had great possessions. I understand after working so hard for so long to obtain what it is you have it can be hard to give it up at a moment's notice. Am I saying it's wrong to have? Absolutely not! Jesus simply presented the individual with a *choice*, which to the individual, it became a *challenge*, based on *his* value system.

As I challenge each of us, like this individual, some will go away never giving heed to the word of God, neither making the decision to have a change of heart as it relates to their value system. John 6:60, although on another subject, it says, ***"Therefore many of His disciples, when they heard this, said, This is a hard saying; who can understand it?"*** From that many of His disciples went back and walked with Him no more. (verse 66)

Jesus was not teaching that you had to be poor in order to follow Him. However, He was trying to get the rich young ruler, as He does with us, to see the importance of loving Him, who is the giver of all things, rather than loving things. He also challenged him in it to deny himself, which is totally opposite of what the world teaches. Jesus was simply saying that the way to *Life More Abundantly* comes from serving Him and others, rather than serving our own selfish wants and desires. This, for many is a hard saying, as they will never choose to walk in that way.

We've learned through our studies in the book of Acts that it was *after the power* the possession came. Peter said, as I paraphrase... *"Silver and gold I do not have. I don't have any money, but what I do have I give you:* ***"In the Name of Jesus Christ of Nazareth, rise up and walk."*** *(Acts 3:6)*

Peter may not have had money *at that moment*, which is what the impotent man was looking for. Which is what most seek today. However, he did possess the ***power*** and ***ability*** to change this man's entire situation. Peter didn't have what this man wanted per se', but he did have what he needed.

Like most today, what's wanted as opposed to what's needed is a far cry from reality. It was *after* the miracles, signs, wonders and prayers of boldness that wealth came.

> *"And with many other words he testified and exhorted them, saying, Be saved from this perverse generation...Then those who gladly received his word were baptized...Then fear came upon every soul, and many wonders and signs were done through the Apostles."*
> *(Acts 2:40, 41, and 43 Amplified Bible)*

> *"Now the company of believers was of one heart and soul, and not one of them claimed that anything which he possessed was [exclusively] his own, but everything they had was in common and for the use of all. And with great strength and ability and power the apostles delivered their testimony to the resurrection of the Lord Jesus, and great grace (loving-kindness and favor and goodwill) rested richly upon them all. Nor was there a destitute or needy person among them, for as many as were owners of lands or houses*

proceeded to sell them, and one by one they brought (gave back) the amount received from the sales And laid it at the feet of the apostles (special messengers). Then distribution was made according as anyone had need."
(Acts 4:32-37 Amplified Bible)

It was *after* the people *saw* the power of God made *evident* and the *change* it wrought to those they encountered. Then, the people began to *release*, and *let go* of, what they had naturally in their possession, in order for distribution to be made to **all** who had need.

Luke 4:18 declares, "The Spirit of the Lord [is] upon Me, because He has anointed Me to preach the good news to the poor; He has sent Me to announce release to the captives and recovery of sight to the blind, to send forth as delivered those who are oppressed [who are downtrodden, bruised, crushed, and broken down by calamity], To proclaim the accepted and acceptable year of the Lord" [the day when salvation and the free favors of God profusely abound]." (Amplified Bible)

Acts 16: 23-26 says, "And when they had struck them with many blows [them being Paul and Silas], they threw them into prison...But about midnight, as Paul and Silas was praying and singing hymns of praise to God, and the

[other] prisoners were listening to them,
Suddenly there was a great earthquake, so that
the very foundations of the prison were shaken;
and at once all the doors were opened and
everyone's shackles were unfastened."
(Amplified Bible)

Imagine having access to that kind of power not only *residing within* you, for you, but within you to make the difference in the lives of multitudes. What am I saying? **Power is available for change. Prayer is a weapon of warfare for change.** But who's willing to live the life, make the sacrifice, risk the ridicule it takes to have this kind of abundant life at their disposal?

Although the disciples paid a tremendous price, no amount of money could measure up to the true reward of deliverance many received that impacted their lives forever. Jesus paid a tremendous price...Oh but for the joy that was set before Him [you, you and I], He endured the cross, despising the shame!

There is not one person, sharing this experience, that does not know of someone who is bound, not just physically, but mentally, spiritually and emotionally, as well. Who does not need a *God encounter* of *this* kind!

When visiting blindness, it is usually visited in its natural aspect of the eye. However, if viewed in a different light, the vast number of us who have allowed our vision to become blurred, even dim as it relates to our goals, dreams and aspirations, would agree we could use some *"recovery of sight!"*

So, as Jesus so eloquently puts it, though relating at the time to somewhat of a different situation, I shall borrow it relevant to say, **"He who is without,"** [having never been guilty of being bruised, crushed, broken down or hurt by calamity,] **come forth and cast, or throw a stone."** The mere gesture that it's everyone else you wish to present guilty, is a cover up towards you having the same need as the rest of us…The **Life** of God, the **Mercy** of God and the **Power** of God to heal and to make whole all of the broken down areas set up over time in our lives with which we have become comfortable living.

Life has struck us all with many blows. Being struck is one thing…staying there is a horse of a different color. Imagine *everyone's* shackles being loosed…*everything* ever **held up**, **bound**, **tied**, or **brought to a halt** in our lives, being **loosed**! Imagine your loved ones **totally healed**, **delivered** and **made whole** due to a conscious decision on your part to *surrender* your life to Christ!

Today, the world, nor the Body of Christ is seeing enough evident power and life changing experiences. Inasmuch, inhibiting people to solely give their lives over, let alone, release their possessions in order for the church to go forth in kingdom growth and works.

Living life more abundantly takes more than just "living." Living life more abundantly takes living right. Living life more abundantly takes living in accordance to God's word, His way, which by the way, takes obedience and discipline on our part.

> ***Matthew 6:33… "But seek (aim at and strive after) first of all His Kingdom and His righteousness (His way of doing and being right) and then all these things taken together will be given you besides." (Amplified Bible)***

We are not to live by our own definition of what's right in our eyes. We are not to live by this lawless living of today where anything goes, and everything is accepted. This world has become so corrupt; evil has been accepted as the normal way of life, while good is being considered as evil. Unfortunately, everybody *is not* saved, and everyone *is not* going to Heaven!

> ***Matthew 6:24-25: No one can serve two masters; for either he will hate the one and love the other, or he will stand by and be devoted to***

the one and despise and be against the other. You cannot serve God and mammon (deceitful riches, money, possessions, or whatever is trusted in). Therefore, I tell you, stop being perpetually uneasy (anxious and worried) about your life, what you shall eat or what you shall drink; or about your body, what you shall put on. Is not life greater [in quality] than food, and the body [far above and more excellent] than clothing?"
(Amplified Bible)

Romans 8:19, 22 and 23… "For the whole creation waits expectantly and longs earnestly for God's sons to be made known [waits for the revealing]. We know that the whole creation has been moaning together in the pains of labor until now. And not only the creation, but we ourselves too…"

We're in pain! It's like a woman in labor. She knows the baby's right there. But, *being close,* and *actually delivering,* is something altogether different. I'm a mom, and I can relate and know someone out there will relate with me. There's nothing like waiting in expectation and nothing is happening. The contractions are there, the water has broken, but that baby ain't coming. And you are left with no choice but to wait. You're left with the pangs, the contractions, and the labor of potential birth, only to become weary in the process, with no strength left to PUSH when the *actual time* does come.

We are the Body of Christ. We know what it is we've been given. We know what's been made accessible to us: The Name and authority of Jesus, the Blood of Jesus, the power of God through His word and the Holy Spirit. It's all right there, yet for whatever reason, many of us seem incapable of bringing forth. Thank God we are admonished in His word to be not weary…for we *shall reap* if we faint not. One thing I love about God is, no matter where we find ourselves, it's never a place from where we can't come up. He always knows where we are, and *He* remains faithful to deliver. We must begin to *take charge* and not allow the world to dictate to us who we are, what our value is and WHO our God is.

Stop allowing the world to push forth their image and their agenda of what the church is suppose to look like. I challenge believers everywhere to *stand up* and birth the church of the True and Living God!

Ephesians 4:4 says, [There is one body, and one Spirit, even as ye are called in one hope of your calling; One Lord, one faith, one baptism, One God and Father of all, who [is] above all, and through all, and in you all.

Genesis 11:6 says, "And the Lord said, Behold the people [is] one, and they have all one language; and this they began to do: and now nothing will be restrained from them, that they have imagined to do."

However, we can not do this with everyone doing their own thing. *"Now we <u>beseech</u> you, brethren, by the coming of our Lord Jesus Christ, and by our gathering together unto Him, That ye be not soon shaken in mind, or be troubled, neither by spirit, nor by word, nor by letter as from us, as that the day of Christ is at hand. Let no man deceive you by any means: for that day shall not come, except there come a falling away first, and that man of sin be revealed, the son of perdition; Who opposeth and exalteth himself above all that is called god, or that is worshipped; so that he as god sitteth in the temple of God, showing himself that he is god. Remember ye not, that, when I was yet with you, I told you these things? And now ye know what withholdeth that he might be revealed in his time. For the mystery of <u>iniquity</u> doth already work: only He who now letteth will let, until He be taken out of the way.*
"And then shall that <u>wicked one</u> be revealed, whom the Lord shall consume with the spirit of His mouth, and shall destroy with the brightness of His coming: Even <u>him</u>, whose coming is after the working of satan with all power and signs and lying wonders, And with all

deceivableness of unrighteousness in them that perish; because they received not the love of the truth, that they might be saved. And for this cause God shall send them strong delusion, that they should believe a lie: That they all might be damned who believed not the truth, but had pleasure in unrighteousness. "
(2 Thessalonians 2:1-12)

After all, whose church is it anyway?

"But we are bound to give thanks alway to God for you, brethren beloved of the Lord, because God hath from the beginning chosen you to salvation through sanctification of the Spirit and belief of the truth: Whereunto He called you by our gospel, to the obtaining of the glory of our Lord Jesus Christ. Therefore, brethren, stand fast, and hold the traditions which ye have been taught, whether by word, or our epistle. Now our Lord Jesus Christ himself, and God, even our Father, which hath loved us, and hath given us everlasting consolation and good hope through grace, Comfort your hearts, and stablish you in every good word and work. "
(2 Thessalonians 2:13-17)

St. Mark 3:24-25 and 1 Corinthians 1:13 both give reference to a house divided being unable to stand.

"And if a kingdom be divided against itself, that kingdom cannot stand. And if a house be divided against itself, that house cannot stand."

"Is Christ divided? was Paul crucified for you? or were ye baptized in the name of Paul?"

If the enemy understands this principle and seems to master the concept of uniting *for the sole purpose* to fulfill *his* agenda, what prevents the church, which is called to *unity* and *oneness*, from uniting to fulfill the purpose of God whom we say we all love and serve? Things that make you go… ***hmmmmm***.

How is it that there are churches all over the world on every corner and block you turn? Yet, the only thing we seem to master is division and confusion with little or no real evident affect of the church on the world?

Matthew 12:33-35 admonishes us to either make the tree good, and its fruit good; or else make the tree corrupt and his fruit corrupt: for the tree is known by [his] fruit.

I will continue to go to the scriptures and keep the word ever before *you.* It is only as *we look into* the perfect law of liberty shall *we* be blessed in our deeds, according to James 1:5. For too long we have slowly allowed the word, our God and the things pertaining to Him, to subtly be taken out. Therefore, the very *source*, *substance* and **Answer** to the ills of our world have been removed from amongst us, and out of several situations in which we could possibly find ourselves involved.

Notice, the scripture said, a house divided. He did not say *houses* divided can't stand. From the beginning, there was only meant to be One house...The House of God. It has always been in the heart of God, and the intent of God, for the Body of Christ to be one body. It wasn't intended for everybody to walk according to their own way. Nor was it intended for all these individual tents and tabernacles to be erected to the glory of man. **We are the temple!**

How can we, being the temple, having the Holy Ghost *in us*, not be able to come together, but expect to *bring to us* an entire world that is lost and dying? It ain't happening!

Once again, as it is written, *Mark 7:6-9, 13-23 says, "He answered and said unto them, Well hath Esaias prophesied of you hypocrites, as it is written, this people honoureth me with [their] lips, but their heart is far from me…making the work of God of none effect through your tradition, which ye have delivered; and many such like things do ye."*

Many such things men do, such as build buildings, is fine. While building, make sure it's not in the name of the Lord for your own selfish gain. While building, make sure it's not to build your brand, or a bigger name for yourself. While all this building is going on, where is our true heart for God and where are the evident works of God? Wrongful acts disguised as the works of God causes the world to view the church in disgust. So, because of this, while trying to convince the world to join the church, the world ain't studding us. We are too scattered, too divided, too opinionated and too proud to lay aside our differences. However, in order to see the works Christ displayed made manifest in and through us, we must start doing things differently.

Respect has been lost. Reverence for the house of the Lord has been lost. The fear of God has been lost and we're just *"having church!"* In scripture, as the Apostles went into regions, they set up **one**

church for that **entire region**. The church of Corinth, the church of Philipi, the church of Galatia, the church at Ephesus, the church in Colosse. They didn't go to a region and decide which one out of 55 in that area they would go to in order to address the people. There was one church where all assembled together.

We're crazy! We've lost sight. We've lost focus. We're about our business, rather than being about the business of The Lord. *Luke 2:49, "And he said unto them, How is it that ye sought me? Wist ye not that I must be about my Father's business? Another scripture, John 4:34: Jesus saith unto them, My meat is to do the will of him that sent me, and to finish his work."*

We're deciding *who* it is we're going to help and *where* it is we will go. Some leaders think, "If you ain't big enough in name or numbers, then you ain't big enough for me to waste my time stopping through to help you."

Just a side note to be aware…the Holy Ghost *informed* Paul as to *where* to go and *who* to help. The Holy Ghost **interrupted** *Paul's agenda* to **impart** *His agenda*. Not only does that take *a life in Christ*, being led by the Spirit of God, but that takes a true heart and *willingness* to do the will of the Lord and to be about His business!

"Now when they had gone throughout Phrygia and the region of Galatia and were forbidden of the Holy Ghost to preach the word in Asia, After they were come to Mysia, they assayed to go into Bithynia: but the Spirit suffered them not. And they passing by Mysia came down to Troas.
And a vision appeared to Paul in the night; There stood a man of Macedonia, and prayed him, saying, Come over into Macedonia, and help us. And after he had seen the vision, immediately we endeavoured to go into Macedonia, assuredly gathering that the Lord had called us for to preach the gospel unto them." (Acts 16:6-10)

Yes, we are still talking about *life and that more abundantly*! Sadly, church has pretty much become a political battlefield. An arena for some who are Pastors, Bishops, clergy and the like, to see who has the most influence to put one up and take one down at the drop of a word. *Newsflash…* It is God who judges! *Psalms 75:6-7: "For promotion cometh neither from the east, nor from the west, nor from the south. But God is the judge: he putteth down one, and setteth up another."* Be careful people of God, for many will say, Lord, did we not …in Your name… and He will say, Depart from Me, I <u>never</u> knew you.

What frightens me of this saying is, the Lord did not say He was aware at some point, rather **He**

never knew! Please don't let this be God's encounter of you after working so hard to obtain so much. The grand thing about our God is that it is *never too late to turn*!

Let's work on creating within us a clean heart and renewing within us the *right spirit*. Not only do we need to come together, but we need to get it together and quick! No longer do we need to be out for ourselves, but also for the increase of others. No longer should we say, "I got mine...you get yours" mentality! That not only affects us as the church, but the mass majority is suffering, whether we believe it or not. For the whole world is waiting!

> *"For we know that the whole creation groaneth and travaileth in pain together until now. And not only they, but ourselves also, which have the firstfruits of the Spirit, even we ourselves groan within ourselves, waiting for the adoption, to wit, the redemption of our body. For we are saved by hope: but hope that is seen is not hope: for what a man seeth, why doth he yet hope for? But if we hope for that we see not, then do we with patience wait for it.*
> *Likewise, the Spirit also helpeth our infirmities: for we know not what we should pray for as we ought: but the Spirit itself maketh intercession for us with groanings which cannot be uttered. And he that searcheth the hearts*

knoweth what is the mind of the Spirit, because he maketh intercession for the saints according to the will of God. And we know that all things work together for good to them that love God, to them who are the called according to his purpose. For whom he did foreknow, he also did predestinate to be conformed to the image of his Son, that he might be the firstborn among many brethren. Moreover, whom he did predestinate, them he also called: and whom he called, them he also justified: and whom he justified, them he also glorified. What shall we then say to these things?

"If God be for us, who can be against us? He that spared not his own Son, but delivered him up for us all, how shall he not with him also freely give us all things?"
(Acts 8:22-32)

Now that's *LIFE*.

Now is the acceptable time. Now is salvation closer than we think. Now is the time for us to right that which is wrong. Until we, as the people of God humble ourselves and pray, seek His face, turn from our wicked ways, will we begin to see things God's way. Only when we begin to do it His way, will we see the Body of Christ advance in the earth as intended. Only then, can we move forth in the "greater works than these…" spoken concerning us, in St. John 14:12.

For many, making this decision may be one of the hardest ever having to be made. Nevertheless, I challenge believers everywhere to move from a life of *self-absorbed* abundance, to life and *that* more abundantly!

...*Who* are you living for? Are you *living life*, or just *plain living*?

"EVILS" UNAWARE

In the previous chapters, we've discussed, God's way of doing things, in order to have the *God kind* of life and *"that"* [life] more abundantly. In this chapter, we will hear the conclusion of the whole matter, which is my prayer. "Fear God and keep His commandments, which is the whole duty of man."

While many of us are trying to obtain stuff first, we are becoming sidetracked *unaware*. Prosperity and riches come not without the price of evil being present: *"For the love of money is a root of all evils; it is through this craving that some have been led astray and have wandered from the faith and pierced themselves through with many acute [mental] pangs." (1 Timothy 6:10 Amplified Bible)*

St. Luke 12:15-21 conveys, "And he said unto them, Take heed, and beware of covetousness: for a man's life consisteth not in the abundance of the things which he possesseth. And he spake a parable unto them, saying, "The ground of a certain rich man brought forth plentifully: And he thought within himself, saying, What shall I do, because I have no room where to bestow my fruits? And he said, This will

I do: I will pull down my barns, and build greater; and there will I bestow all my fruits and my goods. And I will say to my soul, Soul, thou hast much goods laid up for many years; take thine ease, eat, drink, and be merry. But God said unto him, Thou fool, this night thy soul shall be required of thee: then whose shall those things be, which thou hast provided? So, is he that layeth up treasure for himself, and is not rich toward God."

We have been driven with fervor and passion towards the *things we've desired.* All the while, we have *taken our ease* from the very things of the Lord. We have lost the very purpose as to *why* we have been *allowed* to obtain such wealth.

Our priorities have switched. While we eat, drink, and be merry, we believe that the small amount of time spent in church is enough for our soul to be at ease. We witness its devastations when we look on our city blocks, street corners, neighborhood stores, adjacent communities, school systems, government offices, business districts, entertainment and sports arenas. And, more importantly, as we open the doors to enter the vestibules of our own homes.

God's heart is screaming! God's Kingdom is suffering! God's people are waiting! The world is waiting. The world is waiting to be changed. The world is waiting to be made whole. The world is waiting to rise up and walk in power, in authority, and dominion, in every area of life. People are going after things that only satisfy *for a moment*. They are **empty, void** (replacing it with shallow thrills), and **alone**. People are crying in the dark, while wearing a multiplicity of masks in the light. Many are famished, malnourished and impoverished. People have little to no supply to give. Individuals are grabbing as much as they can for themselves, too focused on fixing *their stuff*.

We have, whether we're aware or *unaware,* messed up this thing called *Christianity*. We're doing what we want instead of doing what we have been **commissioned** to do.

Let's review what we have at our disposal. We have the **Life** of God, the **Word** of God, the **Spirit** of God, the **Anointing** of God, the **Bread** of Life, and the **Blood** of Jesus, not to mention the **gift** of the Spirit! In other words, the very **substance** of what people need can and should be found within us. But, as God is saying one thing, we are on the defensive saying, "Did we not prophesy in Thy name? And in Thy name do many wonderful works?"

"Ye shall know them by their fruits. Do men gather grapes of thorns, or figs of thistles? Even so every good tree bringeth forth good fruit; but a corrupt tree bringeth forth evil fruit. A good tree cannot bring forth evil fruit, neither can a corrupt tree bring forth good fruit. Every tree that bringeth not forth good fruit is hewn down, and cast into the fire. Wherefore by their fruits ye shall know them. Not everyone that saith unto Me, Lord, Lord, shall enter into the kingdom of heaven; but he that doeth the will of my Father which is in heaven. Many will say to Me in that day, Lord, Lord, have we not prophesied in thy name? and in thy name have cast out devils? and in thy name done many wonderful works? And then will I profess unto them, I never knew you: depart from Me, ye that work iniquity. Therefore whosoever heareth these sayings of Mine, and doeth them, I will liken him unto a wise man, which built his house upon a rock: And the rain descended, and the floods came, and the winds blew, and beat upon that house; and it fell not: for it was founded upon a rock. And every one that heareth these sayings of Mine, and doeth them not, shall be likened unto a foolish man, which built his house upon the sand: And the rain descended, and the floods came, and the winds blew, and beat upon that house; and it fell: and great was the fall of it."
(Matthew 7:16-27)

As we continue to make excuses as to *why* the **real work** of the Kingdom is not made manifest and began to hear more of *what we think* the work is as opposed to *what God expects* out of us, let's keep Isaiah 58: 5-6 in mind.

> *"Is it such a fast that I have chosen? A day for a man to afflict his soul? is it to bow down his head as a bulrush, and to spread sackcloth and ashes under him? wilt thou call this a fast, and an acceptable day to the Lord? Is not this the fast that I have chosen? to loose the bands of wickedness, to undo the heavy burdens, and to let the oppressed go free, and that ye break every yoke?"*

Lord, did we not *grace* you with our presence in church today? Did I not stay up *all night* praying? Did not eight people join during alter call *on my song*? Only to find the answer to all of these and many more to be, "Depart from Me all ye *workers* of iniquity…" Yes, we're *working*. We are doing *"things,"* and in our eyes and in the eyes of many, *making a difference*. We *are* working, but what is it that we *are* working? Is it the works of *Him* that sent us, or is it the works of *deception, manipulation* and *vain glory*? This only indicates [to me] that there are a lot of *"things"* being done both in the church and outside of the church… things in our personal lives, and in the lives of others, all in the name of Jesus. This may or may not merit God's approval. That's scary, isn't it? Or, perhaps just plain *evil, unaware*? It concerns me that someone can consciously *believe* they are doing everything right. However, they are unaware they are headed for disaster.

Unawares:

If they have called the master of the house Beelzebub, how much more?

> *"Then a demon-possessed man who was blind and mute was brought to Jesus, and He healed him, so that the mute man both spoke and saw. All the people wondered in amazement, and said, Could this be the Son of David (the Messiah)? But the Pharisees heard it and said, This man casts out demons by [the help of] Beelzebul (Satan) the prince of the demons. Knowing their thoughts Jesus said to them, Any kingdom that is divided against itself is being laid to waste; and no city or house divided against itself will [continue to] stand. If Satan casts out Satan [that is, his demons], he has become divided against himself and disunited; how then will his kingdom stand? But if it is by the Spirit of God that I cast out the demons, then the kingdom of God has come upon you [before you expected it]."*
> *(Matthew 12:22-26, 28)*

"And, when they came to Nachon's threshing floor, Uzzah put forth his hand to the ark of God and took hold of it; for the oxen shook it. And the anger of the Lord was kindled against Uzzah; and God smote him there for his error; and there he died by the ark of God."
(2 Samuel 6:6-7)

"Let destruction come upon him at unawares; and let his net that he hath hid catch himself: into that very destruction let him fall."
(Psalms 35:8)

"Enter not into the path of the wicked, and go not in the way of evil [men]. Avoid it, pass not by it, turn from it, and pass away... For they sleep not, except they have done mischief; and their sleep is taken away, unless they cause [some] to fall."
(Proverbs 4:14-16)

"With her much fair speech she caused him to yield, with the flattering of her lips she forced him. Till a dart strike through his liver; as a bird hasteth to the snare, and knoweth not that it [is] for his life. Let not thine heart decline to her ways, go not astray in her paths. For she hath cast down many wounded: yea, many strong [men] have been slain by her. Her house [is] the way to hell, going down to the chambers of death." (Proverbs 7:21, 23, 25-27)

"But beware of men: for they will deliver you up to the councils, and they will scourge you in their synagogues; And ye shall be brought before governors and kings for my sake, for a testimony against them and the Gentiles."
(Matthew 10:17-18)

"And the brother shall deliver up the brother to death, and the father the child: and the children shall rise up against their parents and cause them to be put to death. And ye shall be hated of all men for my name's sake: but he that endureth to the end shall be saved."
(Matthew 10:21-22)

"The disciple is not above his master, nor the servant above his lord. It is enough for the disciple that he be as his master, and the servant as his lord. of his household?"
(Matthew 10:24-25)

"And fear not them which kill the body but are not able to kill the soul: but rather fear him which is able to destroy both soul and body in hell." (Matthew 10: 28)

"...Master, all these have I observed from my youth...One thing thou lackest: go thy way, sell whatsoever thou hast, and give to the poor, and thou shalt have treasure in heaven: and come, take up the cross, and follow me...And he was

sad at that saying, and went away grieved: for he had great possessions." (Mark 10:20-22)

"Then Peter began to say unto him, Lo, we have left all, and have followed thee...And Jesus answered and said, Verily I say unto you, There is no man that hath left house, or brethren, or sisters, or father, or mother, or wife, or children, or lands, for my sake, and the gospel's, But he shall receive an hundredfold now in this time, houses, and brethren, and sisters, and mothers, and children, and lands, with persecutions; and in the world to come eternal life."
(Mark 10: 28-30)

"And take heed to yourselves, lest at any time your hearts be overcharged with surfeiting, and drunkenness, and cares of this life, and [so] that day come upon you unawares. For as a snare shall it come on all them that dwell on the face of the whole earth. Watch ye therefore, and pray always, that ye may be accounted worthy to escape all these things that shall come to pass, and to stand before the Son of man."
(Luke 21:34-36)

"There hath no temptation taken you but such as is common to man: but God [is] faithful, who will not suffer you to be tempted above that ye are able; but will with the temptation also make a way to escape, that ye may be able to bear [it]. Wherefore, my dearly beloved, flee from idolatry.

I speak as to wise men; judge ye what I say."
(1 Corinthians 10:13-15)

"And that because of false brethren unawares brought in, who came in privily to spy out our liberty which we have in Christ Jesus, that they might bring us into bondage."
(Galatians 2:4)

"For before that certain came from James, he did eat with the Gentiles: but when they were come, he withdrew and separated himself, fearing them which were of the circumcision."
(Galatians 2:12)

"And the other Jews dissembled likewise with him; insomuch that Barnabas also was carried away with their dissimulation."
(Galatians 2:13)

"But when I saw that they walked not uprightly according to the truth of the gospel, I said unto Peter before [them] all, If thou, being a Jew, livest after the manner of Gentiles, and not as do the Jews, why compellest thou the Gentiles to live as do the Jews? Knowing that a man is not justified by the works of the law, but by the faith of Jesus Christ, even we have believed in Jesus Christ, that we might be justified by the faith of Christ, and not by the works of the law: for by the works of the law shall no flesh be justified."
(Galatians 2:14)

But if, while we seek to be justified by Christ, we ourselves also are found sinners, [is] therefore Christ the minister of sin? God forbid. For if I build again the things which I destroyed, I make myself a transgressor. For I through the law am dead to the law, that I might live unto God. I am crucified with Christ: nevertheless I live; yet not I, but Christ liveth in me: and the life which I now live in the flesh I live by the faith of the Son of God, who loved me, and gave himself for me. I do not frustrate the grace of God: for if righteousness [come] by the law, then Christ is dead in vain; For the mystery of iniquity doth already work: only he who now letteth [will let], until he be taken out of the way."
(Galatians 2:17-21)

"And then shall that Wicked be revealed, whom the Lord shall consume with the spirit of his mouth, and shall destroy with the brightness of his coming: [Even him], whose coming is after the working of Satan with all power and signs and lying wonders, And with all deceivableness of unrighteousness in them that perish; because they received not the love of the truth, that they might be saved. And for this cause God shall send them strong delusion, that they should believe a lie:

That they all might be damned who believed not the truth, but had pleasure in unrighteousness."
(2 Thessalonians 2:8-12)

And [that] they may recover themselves out of the snare of the devil, who are taken captive by him at his will."
(2 Timothy 2:26)

"Let brotherly love continue. Be not forgetful to entertain strangers: for thereby some have entertained angels unawares. Remember them that are in bonds, as bound with them; [and] them which suffer adversity, as being yourselves also in the body. Marriage [is] honourable in all, and the bed undefiled: but whoremongers and adulterers God will judge. [Let your] conversation [be] without covetousness; [and be] content with such things as ye have: for he hath said, I will never leave thee, nor forsake thee. So that we may boldly say, The Lord [is] my helper, and I will not fear what man shall do unto me. Remember them which have the rule over you, who have spoken unto you the word of God: whose faith follow, considering the end of [their] conversation. Jesus Christ the same yesterday, and today, and forever. Be not carried about with divers and strange doctrines. For [it is] a good thing that the heart be established with grace; not with meats, which

have not profited them that have been occupied
therein; For there are certain men crept in
unawares, who were before of old ordained to
this condemnation, ungodly men, turning the
grace of our God into lasciviousness, and denying
the only Lord God, and our Lord Jesus Christ."
(Hebrews 13:1-9)

"I will therefore put you in remembrance, though
ye once knew this, how that the Lord, having
saved the people out of the land of Egypt,
afterward destroyed them that believed not.
And the angels which kept not their first estate,
but left their own habitation, he hath reserved in
everlasting chains under darkness unto the
judgment of the great day.
Even as Sodom and Gomorrha, and the cities
about them in like manner, giving themselves
over to fornication, and going after strange flesh,
are set forth for an example, suffering the
vengeance of eternal fire.
Likewise also these [filthy] dreamers defile the
flesh, despise dominion, and speak evil of
dignities. Yet Michael the archangel, when
contending with the devil he disputed about the
body of Moses, durst not bring against him a
railing accusation, but said, The Lord rebuke
thee. But these speak evil of those things which
they know not: but what they know naturally, as
brute beasts, in those things they corrupt
themselves. Woe unto them! for they have gone

in the way of Cain and ran greedily after the error of Balaam for reward, and perished in the gainsaying of Core. These are spots in your feasts of charity, when they feast with you, feeding themselves without fear: clouds [they are] without water, carried about of winds; trees whose fruit withereth, without fruit, twice dead, plucked up by the roots; Raging waves of the sea, foaming out their own shame; wandering stars, to whom is reserved the blackness of darkness forever.
And Enoch also, the seventh from Adam, prophesied of these, saying, Behold, the Lord cometh with ten thousands of his saints,
To execute judgment upon all, and to convince all that are ungodly among them of all their ungodly deeds which they have ungodly committed, and of all their hard [speeches] which ungodly sinners have spoken against him.
These are murmurers, complainers, walking after their own lusts; and their mouth speaketh great swelling [words], having men's persons in admiration because of advantage.
But, beloved, remember ye the words which were spoken before of the apostles of our Lord Jesus Christ; How that they told you there should be mockers in the last time, who should walk after their own ungodly lusts.
These be they who separate themselves, sensual, having not the Spirit."
(Jude verses 5-19)

In the same manner it took for us to perfect the sins (the act) through the nature (sin), likewise, it will take time and commitment to perfecting the new creation, which is through Christ Jesus. If we were honest, the acts of our nature have led us down various roads of desolation and destruction. In order to see true change, true REPENTANCE must take place. For change to truly take place, one must not be ashamed of Gospel, for it is the power of God unto salvation. In like manner, with the help of the Holy Spirit, change can and will occur to turn our lives back in the direction intended from the beginning.

*...Evil **Unaware** or just plain evil?*

MORE THAN A *MILLIONHEIR*

Well Beloved, we have approached the closing chapter of this book. This chapter will allow us to take inventory of how we've viewed ourselves. This chapter will reiterate what we have been given, what's on the inside of us and how we've allowed the stigmas of society to define and affect the Church as a whole.

I pray that what has been shared, thus far, has enlightened and thrust you to greater hunger. We have an awesome responsibility as representatives for what has been placed at our disposal to emulate change and manifest Christ in the earth. My continued prayer is that this book is not just *more reading* material deposited on a shelf. Rather, I pray the POWER of God continues to impact your spirit, to change the way we've looked at ourselves, the church and the worlds around us. To God be the Glory!

Let's take our final journey into the word of God and look closer at the life and times of the Acts of the Apostles.

Acts 2:40-45; 5:42 and Matthew 6:33 all show, not only the power, but the importance behind seeking first the Kingdom of God:

"And with many other words did he testify and exhort, saying, Save yourselves from this untoward generation. Then they that gladly received his word were baptized: and the same day there were added unto them about three thousand souls. And they continued steadfastly in the apostles' doctrine and fellowship, and in breaking of bread, and in prayers. And fear came upon every soul: and many wonders and signs were done by the apostles. And all that believed were together and had all things common; And sold their possessions and goods, and parted them to all men, as every man had need. And daily in the temple, and in every house, they ceased not to teach and preach Jesus Christ;
"But seek ye first the kingdom of God, and his righteousness; and all these things shall be added unto you."

Here, we have insight on how the Apostles went *daily* from house to house, *daily* in prayer, *daily* in fellowship and *daily* giving themselves to the word of God. We learn how having an appetite that consists *daily* of what's good, manufactures knowledge, nurturing, community, true fellowship, healing and growth.

A routine along the lines of the above regimen, causes a movement that transforms people from one place to another. The type of environment discussed in previous scripture, transforms one degree of mindset to a different level of thinking, living and being. Breaking of bread, in their day, both naturally and spiritually, puts to shame the very narcissistic, grandiose and recreational services of our day.

What the Apostles grasped and enforced was authentic and powerful. In taking the time and sharing in the fellowship of breaking down the word, this allowed them to gain understanding for application. This understanding aided the people against the wiles of any force of darkness. Without question, understanding is what's needed to combat the lawless, relentless, self-destructive society we have taken part in bringing about.

The Apostles communed and continued steadfastly in the doctrine and fellowship, and in breaking of bread, and in prayers (Acts 2:42). They understood that **ONLY** as they walked with Jesus, would they have victory over the various challenges they experienced on a day to day basis.

The Apostles, or disciples at that time, witnessed first-hand, by *walking with* the Lord, His *life*, His *death*, His *burial*, His *resurrection* and His *ascension*. In other words, they experienced **His**

life and learned *how* not to live a life of **religion, tradition,** and **routine** in order to overcome **challenge** and **controversy**. By doing so, they overcame victoriously. They experienced **His death** and was *determined* they could overcome not only dead situations, but things that seemingly could kill or *appear* to *"take the life out of them.* They experienced **His resurrection** and realized there was nothing they couldn't rise above when met with His Life, faith and ability to conquer and triumph over it all. They experienced **His ascension** and became adamant to face any detriment with power and might from on high.

They were a testament to the way He *constantly* and *consistently* gave Himself to the Father: to His purpose and to His will *only*. This type of giving from our Lord and Savior provoked change in the lives of the Apostles. This type of lifestyle can and will provoke a greater determination, responsibility and accountability in the lives of those who are *willing* to give themselves wholly and completely over to His way of life. In turn, this type of life will yield the kind of fruit demonstrated by the Apostles.

The Apostles understood that their lives had to **duplicate** the life Jesus Christ lived. They understood that their lives had to **reflect** the life of the Lord they professed Him to be. They lived to **move** in the direction of Him in whom *they agreed* to follow in order to see the miracles, signs and wonders that Christ Himself displayed.

Jesus, HIMSELF, went from city to city, and from synagogue to synagogue, into several regions and forbidden territories. He sat amongst teachers and doctors of the law, co-mingling with sinners, to promote change, without being influenced by their sins. Comparing Jesus' works to ours – as we sit amongst and co-mingle with sinners, seemingly, we are more influenced. In addition, it appears we have little to no dealings with those who are sick and *dis-eased.*

The majority of people, if asked, and were honest, would prefer *"quick results,"* as opposed to a process. We would that all our problems dissolve in a day. How soon we forget that it took a lifetime of wrong decisions and rebellion to bring us to the place we are now. Perhaps, it may equally take close to a lifetime to bring us out.

"And Jesus looking upon them sayeth, With men, this is impossible, but not with God: for with God, all things are possible."
(Mark 10:27)

"Jesus said unto him, If thou canst believe, all things are possible to him that believeth."
(Mark 8:23)

The questions then become…are we willing to submit ourselves to countless hours in the word of God and in prayer? Are we willing to yield to God-fearing believers, who follow Christ and not the traditions of men, which makes the word of God not effective? Are we willing to submit ourselves to endless mentors, mothers of Zion, fathers in the Gospel, and men and women of God, and trust that it is the very counsel of God for our lives?

In the Amplified version of Mark 7:13 says, *"So you nullify the [authority of the] the word of God [acting as if it did not apply] because of your tradition which you have handed down [through the elders]. And you do many such things as that."*

And, by the way…every preacher ain't crooked and every praying man and woman of God ain't in it for themselves! There are still men and women of God left with integrity, character and the heart of God. There are still believers who are full of faith, the Holy Spirit and the fear of the Lord.

What are we willing to give up, to experience true God encounters and real change? Our lives, and the lives of our children, are dependent upon it. There should be, if not a genuine concern, a subconscious thought regarding the direction to which most individuals are headed.

Jesus *DECLARED*, upon this rock I will build my church and the gates of hell shall not prevail against it. Don't allow hell, demonic forces, nor powers of darkness to invade, trespass or illegally enter your sphere of influence or space. You have been given power over **ALL** the power of the enemy. Begin **DECLARING**! Begin to **CRUSH** every intent and every attempt of the enemy concerning your entire life. Begin speaking over your own life. Begin speaking over the lives of your children. Begin speaking over your marriage. Begin speaking over your household. Begin speaking over your family and your future! Pray. Ask for help. Find someone to whom you can submit. Do not be afraid of the word "submit." It's just another tool that has been abused and improperly taught. God *can* and *will* lead and guide us by **His Spirit**. Remember, *"Wisdom is the principle thing; therefore, get wisdom: and with all thy getting, get understanding." (Proverbs 4:7)* Safety is found in a <u>multitude</u> of ways and people. *Proverbs 11:14 warns, "Where no counsel is, the people fall: but in the multitude of counsellors there is safety."*

At some point, it must be realized that mistakes of the past are just that…mistakes. What you have done, does not define who you really are. However, losing trust in all things and most people can be a detriment to one's sanity and health. Doing things the same way, yet expecting different results, is what many define as insanity. Sooner, rather than later, I pray we awake to the reality that *"something has to give," "things have got to change,"* and *"there has to be more to life than this!"*

Realizations, as such, passionately push us in the direction of change and productivity. Nevertheless, this change must begin with us...change that begin in our thoughts, in our way of thinking and in how we do things. It further reflects through the lens of how we've viewed the entire forecast of our lives, and the way we've seen and perceived things. Our way of thinking must change, and contrary to popular belief, no one else is to blame. ***"But let this mind be in you, which was also in Christ Jesus." (Philippians 2:5)*** It all begins with the *re*newing of *your* mind!

As we read throughout the word of God, for a time, those who followed Christ appeared unable to grasp the concepts He intended via parables and countless examples. They watched daily as they attempted to model themselves according to the patterns set in motion. They listened to His dealings amongst the Scribes and sinners, marveling at the confidence which exuded from Him. Regardless what people group He found Himself in the midst of, He challenged and affected change in all whom He encountered.

The principles and practices that boggled the minds and disturbed the spirits of many a *"religious folk,"* worked an exceeding and eternal weight of glory for the Apostles.

"For our light affliction, which is but for a moment, worketh for us a far more exceeding and eternal weight of glory; While we look not at the things which are seen, but at the things which are not seen: for the things which are seen are temporal; but the things which are not seen are eternal." (2 Corinthians 4:17)

We too, as the Apostles, can admit to countless challenges, struggles and attempts to model ourselves after Christ as it relates to our walk with the Lord. However, without question or much argument, we also can agree it will take a lifetime of continuous yielding, surrender and discipline.

Will this type of lifestyle come without fail? Absolutely not! Will it be easy and flawless? Absolutely not! But, it **will** and **can** be attainable as we determine to see our lives and the lives of those around us changed, set free and delivered. The breaking down of all barriers of religion and watching the Glory of The Lord be revealed amongst us, as with the Apostles, to me, is worth every bit of affliction!

Reflecting on the life of Peter, he too failed on many occasions. He also made mistakes he regretted afterwards, and furthermore, had moments that caused him to hang his head in shame, disappointment and doubt, wondering if he would ever "*get it right.*"

Moments caused Peter to look around and wonder, "*Where are the promises?*" Moments which made circumstances scream louder than reality, caused him to go back to previous ways of doing things. Moments like these made him responsible for bringing others back to the very things they left in the past. If anyone says influence does not play a major role in the decision-making of others, think again!

We can safely conclude, when looking at everything that took place in and around Peter, both naturally and emotionally, it would have been easy for him to "*give up*" and "*throw in the towel.*" He endured hardship as a good soldier.

"But, thanks be unto God, which always causeth us to triumph in Chist, and maketh manifest the savour of His knowledge by us in every place."
(2 Corinthians 2:14)

In viewing this notable portion of scripture, notice, it's **only** in Christ. The victory is **only** in knowing that **His knowledge** of the whole ordeal **super-cedes** knowledge of our tunneled vision. The victory *only* comes as we realize no matter what we find ourselves faced with, we **know** Christ is *in us*, *with us*, *for us* and He's *on our side,* as we are *never* alone in Him!

Jesus knew, despite Peter's rollercoaster ride of events, that when he was *"converted"* from what he was, to what we know him to be throughout the remainder of the acts of the Apostles, the failures of the past could not compare to the triumphs of his future. When Peter was *"converted,"* not just saved, not just a follower – **converted** – he not only strengthened the brethren, but he walked in an authority, boldness and power that even his *shadow* healed! What failure can compare to this type of power?

The failures of the past matter not. The mistakes of our present time matter not. What mattered was Peter *became* converted! What mattered was when it counted, everything *given* him, *in him* paid off! What matters to God is our conversion! What matters to God is a conversion from our way to His way; from the power of Satan to the power God. What matters is the *application* of things that have been entrusted over to us.

I know that *in the moment,* and at that time, it's hard to see, understand, believe and know that the promise *is* to us and to our children. I know that *in it*, it looks more cloudy than clear, and more complicated than what it appears.

If we can believe, hold fast to our faith and trust God, we will see our lives changed…our children transformed and the Body of Christ will take on the very nature, posture, position and power that God intended before the foundation of the world!

"Faithful [is] He that calleth you, who also will do [it]."
(1 Thessalonians 5:24 Amplified Bible)

Ladies and gentlemen, brothers and sisters, when we determine that we have wasted enough time, things will begin to *shift* in the direction of changing lives - including our own.

Most are familiar with the term, *"prodigal son."* Aligning with this particular story, we, too, must *come to ourselves.* We have slopped with the pigs of society long enough, making a mess of things. *Let us also return home, realizing more is waiting for us there than what the enemy made appear to be waiting elsewhere!* When we get angry enough with a wretched past and make room for a rich future, we'll begin putting all the slop of life out of our lives, which is keeping us dirty and distant from our *true destinies*!

We must recognize the weight of riches *entrusted* to us, and the wealth of inheritance on the inside of us. This type of wealth is far greater than any amount of money or fame. Once this is understood, we, like Peter, will also be able to walk into regions only dreamed of and experience depths of anointing only read about!

Only when we turn our attention back to the **True** and **Living** God, the **Only Wise God**, our Father, who art in Heaven, will we begin to change the world. This is good news worth getting excited about! The hours you spend in prayer will pay off! Time spent in His presence and in His word will pay off! Fellowship with the saints and service unto the Lord, is not in vain!

This is that which caused so many to be added to the church daily!

This is that which caused their *works* and their *acts* to be great!

This is that which caused them to be Giants in the Holy Ghost!

> They took the time.
> They recognized the importance.

They recognized that **after** all of *"their way,"* there wasn't any other way!

"THE MAKING OF A MILLION*HEIR*"
In Word,
In Prayer,
In Fellowship...*DAILY*

They recognized that it had to be a *surrendering of their will* in order to receive His will.

There is so much work to be done. Not in and of ourselves, but *through Christ* who strengtheneth us.

In closing, I pray we *do our best* to align our lives with the word of God. In order for us to bring His plans and purposes to past, the word needs to be *established in us* to perfect what God had on His mind concerning us.

I pray we *mirror* our lives to reflect the life of Christ. Exemplifying a life of servitude, becoming *"living epistles"* read of men.

Furthermore, be reminded (as I get 3 closings - inside joke), that everything that took place was a result of what was *already in them*. It was the circumstances of life, along with their trials and errors that brought the anointing to the surface.

Tribulations were the troubles, worries, afflictions, trials, adversities, hardships, tragedies, traumas, setbacks, blows, difficulties, mishaps and misadventures, which formed them into the very person they were always intended to be.

"Many are the afflictions of the righteous: but the Lord delivereth him out of them all."
(Psalms 34:19)

It is written, "But whosoever drinketh of this water that I shall give him shall never thirst; but the water that I shall give him shall be in him a well of water springing up into everlasting life."
(John 4:14)

Are we aware of what's in a well? Are we aware of a well's depth and contents? Are we aware of the maintenance involved in keeping a well clear of debris and its water pure and drinkable?

We are *wells, cisterns* and *containers* that house the very Spirit of God. If we were *more aware* of **who** we were and **what** we had, perhaps we would be more careful as to what we allow inside of us. Perhaps, we would be more conscious of the things we allow to contaminate the flow of God out of our vessels.

Guard your wells! *Guard* your value! *Guard* what *goes in* and *comes up* out of you from all the *contaminates* of life!

Concerning John 4:14, take the time to **know** the *"I,"* **study** the *"I,"* and **commune** with the *"I."* In doing so, you, as the Apostles, will **never be the same, never lack**, never thirst again, never go looking for *cheap thrills* that don't fulfill, nor *temporary fixes* that leave you empty within moments!

So, the next time you profess by faith things that be not as though they were, proclaim before a congregation that money cometh and when it takes too long to come, find a get rich quick remedy or run out to retrieve your favorite numbers on a lottery ticket (oops), think of WHO it is *you say* you represent!

Allow the ***limitless*** wealth of who God is and what He has given to *satiate* your very being. In order to unlock the depth of riches made available to us daily, *get to know*, *spend time with*, and *commune* with The God of *our* salvation. Desire to become all that God wills for your life. That, my Friend, is the making of a true million*heir*!

Because **He is**, and He is on the inside of *you*, doesn't that make you *more than a millionaire*?

Because **He is, we are** and **will always be million*heirs***! No one can put a *true* price on that type of wealth and worth! And what is the *real* value of that kind of *heir*?

So, the next time you're sitting in front of the television set or faced with the question of what it is you want to be, recall this book to memory and know that the wealth of everything you want and need *lies within you*. Therefore, this makes you worth *more* than a million(aire). This makes you an *Heir* with God and a joint-*Heir* with Christ Jesus! Start walking in your "*true wealth*" and begin sharing the type of *'true riches"* that increase you, everything attached to you and everything you touch!

…What have ***you allowed*** to *devalue* **your *true* worth**?

Made in the
USA
Lexington, KY